ACRL Publications in Librarianship no. 52

The Reference Encounter:
Interpersonal Communication in the Academic Library

Marie L. Radford

Association of College and Research Libraries
A Division of the American Library Association
Chicago 1999

The paper used in this publication meets the minimum requirements of American National Standard for Information Sciences–Permanence of Paper for Printed Library Materials, ANSI Z39.48—1992.∞

Library of Congress Cataloging-in-Publication Data
Radford, Marie L.
    The reference encounter : interpersonal communication in the academic library / Marie L. Radford.
        p. cm. -- (ACRL publications in librarianship ; no. 52)
    Includes bibliographical references and index.
    ISBN 0-8389-7951-3 (alk. paper)
    1. Academic libraries--Reference services--United States.
2. Communication in library science--United Stated. I. Title.
II. Series.
Z674.A75 no. 52
[Z675.U5]
020 s--dc21
[025.5'2777'0973]   98-47242

Printed in the United States of America.

03 02 01 00 99   5 4 3 2 1

To Gary and Meg
Mom and Dad
with much love.

Contents

List of Tables

Foreword

During an eighteen-year career as a school and academic librarian, frequently new acquaintances would say to me "You can't be a librarian [because] you're too friendly" or "you smile too much" or even "you're too smart." I found these comments so disconcerting that I began to ask people why they felt this way. Unfortunately, I usually heard a horror story about how they had been mistreated, embarrassed, humiliated, or just plain ignored by a librarian. Usually they hastened to add that not *all* librarians they had known were like this but that they found a smiling, friendly librarian to be out of the ordinary.

I have come to believe that librarians frequently take the interpersonal communication aspects of their work for granted. They work extremely hard to keep up with rapid changes in information sources and electronic information retrieval systems, and to make information accessible to users. Sometimes their reference desks are crowded with users demanding attention and often are understaffed. In their efforts to provide accurate and efficient reference service in a hectic environment, librarians may not realize that the day-to-day, moment-to-moment interpersonal interactions with user's are also critically important.

My interest, kindled by the stories that library users told me, led to a desire to learn more about interpersonal communication and eventually into doctoral research. I began an interdisciplinary program that combined communication, information, and library science specifically to study the interpersonal aspects of the librarian–library user interaction, to understand the dynamics of this process, and ultimately to learn how to improve it. This book is the culmination of eight years of work, and reflects a continuing fascination with the dynamics of interpersonal interaction and a strong desire to expand the body of knowledge about these dynamics and their relationship to user perceptions of librarians. Ultimately, these perceptions determine how effective our reference service is.

Acknowledgements

There are a number of people without whom this book would not have been written. I would like to express my appreciation to all of them. I first want to thank the many anonymous librarian volunteers and library users who generously agreed to be observed and interviewed, and the gracious library administrators at the research sites who welcomed me into their libraries.

I thank the members of my doctoral committee at Rutgers University: Hal Beder, David Carr, Linda Lederman, and Hartmut Mokros. Without their guidance and vision, I would have quickly become lost. Brent Ruben, as committee chair, was a strong and confident mentor. He always enthusiastically supported my work and believed that my study was an important one. Others at Rutgers also need to be recognized: Joan Chabrak for her role in guiding me through the program, and the members of my ABD group for their encouragement and friendship, especially Danny Bernstein for first organizing the ABD group, Pam Snelson, and Wendy Skiba-King.

I am also grateful to my colleagues at the Sarah Byrd Askew Library, William Paterson University of New Jersey who provided ongoing support in the years that I was working full time as an academic librarian while completing the doctorate. Special thanks to Bob Goldberg, Anne Ciliberti, Norma Levy, Jane Hutchison, Jane Bambrick, Kathy Malanga, and Bill Duffy, for offering their friendships and assistance when I needed their superior expertise.

I would also like to thank my colleagues and students at Pratt Institute, especially Dean Seoud M. Matta for continuous support during the past three years during which I totally rewrote the dissertation, transforming it from a scholarly tome into its present (new and improved) version.

Thanks also to my family for their encouragement and faith in my abilities. My parents, Marion and Charles Hein, have provided boundless love and much laughter. I am privileged to have always had them as models of the intellectually curious who, as avid readers and world "gallivanters," are ever excited about learning and living. To the rest of my immediate family, I also offer my appreciation for their gifts of yet more love and laughter: Irene and Charlie Bell, Nicholas and Christine Smolney;

Michael, Tina, Jessica, Jeremiah, Jonathan, and Joel Hein, Theresa and Gerard Stafford-Smith. Also, to my family in England: Howard, Elsie, Mark, and Charlotte Radford, my appreciation for your ongoing encouragement and warm acceptance.

There are no words that can express my love and appreciation for my husband Gary and my daughter Meg. Gary has been a thoughtful mentor, gentle cheerleader, and willing partner in every one of my endeavors. He has helped with every aspect of this book, read and critiqued endless drafts, soothed jagged nerves, and generally put up with me throughout this long process. Thank you Gary. I also want to thank Meg, for her hugs and sunny personality, for reminding me that there is more to life then working, for bringing fun and high drama to my life.

Finally, I want to thank my editor, Steven Wiberly and Hugh Thompson, responsible for the production of ACRL's *Publications in Librarianship* series. I deeply appreciate their efforts. I have come to admire Steve Wiberly for his skills as an editor. He has worked incredibly hard to make sure that this book is of the highest quality and for that I am thankful. In addition, throughout the seemingly endless writing and revising process, he was extremely supportive of me, patient, and willing to listen. I found the process of rewriting my dissertation for the library practitioner to be much more difficult than I had imagined, but Steve provided just the gentle words of encouragement that I needed to hear to keep me going.

I offer my sincere gratitude to all who helped me in the research and writing of this book, especially those who believe in the power and importance of its message.

Chapter 1

Introduction

❦❦ ❦❦ ❦❦ ❦❦ ❦❦ ❦❦ ❦❦ ❦❦ ❦❦

*T*wice, within the first ten pages of his classic text *Introduction to Reference Work,* William Katz discusses the sweeping changes in the reference process that are occurring due to the advances in information retrieval technology and the Internet. He notes, however, that despite these transformational changes, "the goal (the answer to a query) remains a constant. Technology has made it possible to reach that goal faster and with added efficiency."[1] And again: "Because of the rapid changes occurring in information technology, the reference process will continue to change too. But its goal remains the same—to answer questions."[2]

Katz's assertions express a traditional focus on answering questions with efficiency that has characterized reference work. There can be no argument with the statement that the process of reference work is indeed changing, but the research reported in this book challenges the statement that the goal of answering questions "remains a constant."

In volume 2, Katz answers the question posed by James Rettig: "What factors do users weigh most heavily in judging the effectiveness of reference service?"[3] Katz replies, "That's easy. The major factor is a satisfactory answer to their question. The problem is what is 'satisfactory.' Is the average person expecting too much, or too little? Probably too little."[4]

Is this answer correct? Is it "easy" to know what makes an effective reference interaction from the user's point of view? This book challenges the belief that users seek only satisfactory answers to their questions. Rather than imposing a definition of effective reference service, this exploration asked users to define it themselves. The research found that users and librarians differ in their descriptions of goals for reference.

1

In addition, the study found that more than information to answer questions is communicated in the reference interaction. There is also communication about the type of interpersonal relationship being constructed between user and librarian. That means another important goal of reference is *to build positive relationships with library users.* The critical importance of building these positive relationships is what this book is about.

Interpersonal Communication and the Reference Interaction

Interpersonal communication processes are crucial elements in the functioning of libraries in general and in the reference interaction in particular. The academic library of today can be a daunting prospect for the user. In many cases, the old familiar icons of card catalogs and paper indexes have been removed, or perhaps relegated to less visible positions and replaced by rows of computers sprouting myriad wires. Upon entering, one is immediately confronted by a confusing array of workstations with access to online catalogs, complex indexing systems, Internet connections, and a multitude of other electronic resources. Library users may quickly become lost or overwhelmed in this increasingly sophisticated environment of sources and systems.

Many times, students enter the academic library with assignment in hand thinking, "All I need is a few books or articles on my topic. I have ten minutes before my next class; I can just stop in and pick them up or maybe make a quick photocopy or two." When faced with the incredible number and diversity of resources, students (sometimes painfully) come to the realization that what they imagined to be a simple task is not at all simple, nor can it be accomplished in ten minutes. Their initial belief that complex questions are easily answered leave them unprepared for the investment of time and energy needed. Even seasoned faculty members admit that they feel disconcerted by the rapid transformation of the library. Moreover, due to misunderstandings about the state of the art and the impact of budgetary restrictions, all types of users are frequently under the impression that every desired item is available as full text at the push of a printer button.

When library users' attempts to find information fail (or they do not know where to start), they may choose to approach the reference desk. If they do, the librarian becomes the *human* interface or mediator between the library's knowledge base and the information users' need.[5] The critically important moment when users approach and engage the librarian can be the point at which the complexities of the library are gently explained, fears are calmed, and information becomes accessible. Or, if help is withheld, given grudgingly, hurriedly, or in a condescending manner, the encounter becomes the point at which the library appears even more inaccessible. Users can be left feeling confused, frustrated, and sometimes personally defeated or humiliated.

The conviction that an understanding of the interpersonal communication process between librarian and user is vital to the success of the reference encounter has driven the research reported here. Although there has been some research on the interpersonal aspects of reference service, there is much more to be explored and discovered, examined and understood.

The Dual Nature of Interpersonal Communication

There is no doubt that providing users with accurate and complete information whenever possible is a vital function of reference work. However, research in the field of interpersonal communication asserts that *more* than content-oriented information, or correct answers to questions, is being communicated across the reference desk. Librarians are also conveying verbal and nonverbal messages that create a particular kind of relationship with library users.[6] Therefore, the key distinction made in this book is the one between content-oriented and relational dimensions of interpersonal communication. *Content-oriented* dimensions are defined as the report aspect of a message, *what* is being said, the information exchange. *Relational* dimensions signify the command aspect of a message, *how* the message is said, the feelings and attitudes of the participants in an interaction that define their relationship.[7] Relational aspects also reflect the attitudes of the interactants toward one another and toward the encounter.

Two Views of a Reference Interaction

Both content and relational dimensions are present in every instance of interpersonal communication. This dual nature of communication events can be illustrated by the following interaction that took place at a busy reference department in a crowded college library. A student approached the reference desk and asked the librarian for help in locating journal articles on psychology. The librarian directed the student to a computer terminal and briefly showed her how to find articles using the *PsychLit* CD-ROM database. The librarian returned to the reference desk, leaving the student at the computer to continue the database search.

By simply observing this interaction, it is difficult to determine whether it has been successful. Did the student find what she was looking for? Was the librarian satisfied that the student received the needed help? Did both think that this was a successful encounter? The only way to answer these questions is to ask the librarian and student involved. When asked, the two gave contradictory accounts. The student said:

> I felt like she couldn't help me on my subject. Isn't that she didn't know the answer, but I felt that she didn't want to [help]... she looked like she did not know what I was talking about, a blank stare and also almost like irritated.

The librarian, however, gave this account:

> I think it went all right from my viewpoint because I didn't have to really interact too much. She seemed capable, she seemed to know what she was doing. I felt she had found what she wanted because she said she had what she needed. She seemed to be capable of handling it on her own.

According to the librarian's report, this was a successful encounter. The response of the librarian focused on the *content* delivery and believed that the student "had found what she wanted because she said she had what she needed." Yet, within the *relational* dimension the perceptions of the student were expressed in saying, "I felt that she didn't want to [help] . . . she looked like she did not know what I was talking about, a blank stare and also almost like irritated." Even if the correct content information was given and the search could have been completed successfully, the student felt that her interpersonal, relational needs were unsatisfied.

Like other types of interactions, the information exchange between librarian and user *is not and cannot be* free of these relational messages. Messages that are conveyed through verbal and nonverbal dimensions include rapport building, impression management, nonverbal approachability, and empathy. These interpersonal elements affect the ability of the librarian to successfully define the user's question or understand the user's need, to successfully conduct a reference interaction, and to establish a positive relationship.

Focus and Research Questions

Perhaps because of their traditional concern with "getting the right answer" and the accompanying need to maintain an orderly, accessible collection of resources, librarians are often viewed as stern and forbidding.[8] Katz commented:

> Aside from major communication problems with the library system (e.g., catalog, subject headings, index arrangement . . .), the librarian's primary communication problem is himself. Whereas he recognizes the first one, he is loath to recognize the second. And failing to be concerned about image, he rarely takes the time to consider how the average user views his majesty and presence behind the reference desk.[9]

Although there has been recognition of problems within the reference encounter, and recent intriguing research addresses these issues,[10] there continues to be a need for a deeper understanding of its interpersonal dynamics. Marjorie E. Murfin and Gary M. Gugelchuck have described reference service as "poorly mapped-out territory."[11]

This book explores interpersonal issues in the academic reference encounter and adds to our current understanding of this complex process. It focuses on these research questions:

1. What are the perceptions of the participants regarding the relational dimensions of communication between librarian and library user in the reference encounter?

2. What is the relative importance of relational dimensions versus content dimensions of communication as perceived by librarian and library user in the reference encounter?

3. What aspects of the relational dimensions of communication are judged to be of critical importance by librarians and library users in reference encounters?

4. Do those aspects of relational dimensions of communication judged of critical importance by users differ from those of librarians, and if so, how?

Research reported here involved in-depth interviews following twenty-seven reference interactions at academic libraries. Although the sample size is small, this is often the case for qualitative research.[12] This study does not have generalizability of findings as a goal, as would a quantitative study.[13] Its goal is exploratory and descriptive, recognizing that "there is a world of empirical reality out there"[14] (in this case, at the reference desk) and endeavoring to be a part of:

> a long-standing intellectual community [of qualitative research-ers] for which it seems worthwhile to try to figure out collectively how best to talk about the empirical world, by means of incremental, partial improvements in understanding.[15]

The relational model of communication provides the theoretical foundation used to frame a better understanding of the reference process and to integrate the perspectives of both librarian and library user. Before the publication of a journal article based on the author's work, this theoretical model from the field of communication had not been applied to the study of reference service in any published account.[16] Illustrated with the eloquent voices of both library users and librarians, the results help to explain the complex nature of the communication process inherent in reference interactions.

Chapter 2 provides an overview of the library literature on the reference interaction, whereas chapter 3 describes the relevant communication literature. Chapter 4 describes the methodology for selection of sites and subjects, data collection, instruments, and the methodology for three data analysis techniques. Chapters 5 through 8 describe the results of the three analyses. Chapter 9 gives the practical and theoretical implications of this work with recommendations for future study.

Notes

1. William Katz., *Introduction to Reference Work,* Vol. 1, 7th ed. (New York: McGraw Hill, 1997), 7.

2. Ibid., 10.

3. James Rettig, "Reference Research Questions," *RQ* 31 (winter 1991): 169.

4. Katz, *Introduction to Reference Work,* Vol. 2, 255. In fairness to Katz, his well-respected text devotes volume 2 to reference services and processes, and chapter 6, "The Reference Interview," is thorough and well written.

5. See Katz, *Introduction to Reference Work*, and Mary Jo Lynch, "Reference Interviews in Public Libraries" (Ph.D. diss., Rutgers—The State Univ. of New Jersey, 1977).

6. See Paul Watzlawick, Janet Helmick Beavin, and Don D. Jackson, *Pragmatics of Human Communication: A Study of Interactional Patterns, Pathologies, and Paradoxes* (New York: Norton, 1967); Erving Goffman, *The Presentation of Self in Everyday Life* (Garden City, N. Y.: Doubleday Anchor, 1959).

7. See Jurgen Ruesch and Gregory Bateson, *Communication: The Social Matrix of Psychiatry* (New York: Norton, 1951).

8. See Marie L. Radford and Gary P. Radford, "Power, Knowledge, and Fear: Feminism, Foucault and the Stereotype of the Female Librarian," *Library Quarterly* 67 (July 1997); Ellis Mount, "Communication Barriers and the Reference Question," *Special Libraries* 57 (Oct. 1966): 575–78.

9. William Katz, *Introduction to Reference Work*, 2nd ed. (New York: McGraw Hill, 1974), 76.

10. See, for example, Patricia Dewdney and Gillian Michell, "Oranges and Peaches: Understanding Communication Accidents in the Reference Interview," *RQ* 35 (summer 1996): 520–36; Patricia Dewdney and Catherine Sheldrick Ross, "Flying a Light Aircraft: Reference Service Evaluation from the User's Viewpoint," *RQ* 34 (winter 1994): 217–30.

11. Marjorie E. Murfin and Gary M. Gugelchuk, "Development and Testing of a Reference Transaction Assessment Instrument," *College & Research Libraries* 48 (July 1987): 314.

12. See Jana Bradley, "Methodological Issues and Practices in Qualitative Research," *Library Quarterly* 63 (Oct. 1993): 431–49.

13. Thus, no generalizability is sought for these findings, see chapter 9 for limitations.

14. Jerome Kirk and Marc L. Miller, *Reliability and Validity in Qualitative Research* (Beverly Hills, Calif.) Sage, 1986, 11.

15. Ibid., 11.

16. See Marie L. Radford, "Communication Theory Applied to the Reference Encounter: An Analysis of Critical Incidents," *Library Quarterly* 66 (Apr. 1996): 123–37.

Chapter 2

Literature on the
Reference Interaction

☙☙ ☙☙ ☙☙ ☙☙ ☙☙ ☙☙ ☙☙ ☙☙ ☙☙

$\mathcal{F}$ew areas of librarianship have received as much attention as reference, and the literature on the subject is vast. A review of that literature finds long-standing concerns with reference both as information transfer and interpersonal interaction. For an investigator about to undertake an in-depth study of reference librarians and users of reference, a review of the literature identifies factors that can affect the research and issues that may be important to those persons studied. The literature review in this chapter covers the major issues of information transfer and interpersonal aspects of reference. Because interpersonal aspects are the subject of this book, they are covered in much more depth than reference as information transfer. The literature review discusses ways librarians have conceived of reference service and how they have endeavored to improve their interaction with users. It covers studies of librarians *and* users. It includes material from other fields that is relevant and highlights current issues. Finally, it introduces the potential value of communication theory to the study of reference, a topic covered in depth in the next chapter.

Reference as Information Transfer

Benita V. Howell, Edward B. Reeves, and John van Willigen characterize the reference interaction as a "'fleeting encounter,' the rapid establishment of effective communication between two strangers."[1] This "fleeting encounter" has been the subject of a substantial body of literature, much of it taking the view that "effective communication" equals information delivery.[2] Many conceive of the reference encounter as a "fairly straight forward matter of an informed person imparting knowledge to a less informed one."[3] Wayne W. Couch defines the reference interaction as "any interview in which one person is attempting to understand what information another person wants."[4] According to William Young, the reference interview, is: "The interpersonal communication between a reference staff member and a library user to determine the precise information needs of the user."[5] Helen M. Gothberg characterized the interaction as "a 'process' involving tools, service, library organization, and human communication."[6] To Thomas Lee Eichman, the object of the reference librarian was to connect the inquirer's mind to the library's store of knowledge.[7] This view is seconded by Marilyn Domas White: "It is important to recognize that the librarian's primary responsibility in the interview is to resolve the information need, not simply to understand the verbalized question."[8]

Much of the literature that studies the librarian's role in the reference interaction emphasizes the quality of the information exchange. A substantial number of researchers have focused on an evaluation of how well the librarian finds the correct factual answer to specific questions.[9] Many researchers have tried to determine the percentage of "right" answers given by librarians. They have employed proxy users who asked test questions whose answers had been ascertained by those conducting the studies. Their results share a commonality in that:

> they show that the user of a library faces a surprisingly low probability that his factual question will be answered accurately. Overall, the studies tend to support a probability in the range of 50 to 60% with some libraries or groups of libraries doing much worse than this, and a few doing rather better.[10]

The consistency of these findings has resulted in the general acceptance of "the 55% Rule."[11] However, the 1996 "Guidelines for Behavioral Performance of Reference and Information Services Professionals" contend that "Reference performance cannot be measured solely by the accuracy of an answer to a factual question." They remind those who focus on research that led to the 55% Rule that such studies "do not take into account the complex librarian/patron interaction during the reference process."[12]

Writing about the 55% Rule had an enormous impact within the library profession. Emphasis on the information transfer aspects of reference was raised to a new level. Although this book focuses on the other aspects—interpersonal aspects—of the reference encounter, readers should not forget what a large, arguably predominant, role the concept of reference as information transfer has played in the library profession.[13]

Interpersonal Issues in the Reference Interaction

Although virtually all librarians recognize the vital importance of information transfer in reference, there is, at the same time, a long tradition of concern for interpersonal dimensions of reference work. In 1944, for example, Margaret Hutchins produced an influential textbook that gave a chapter to the reference encounter, emphasizing that human interaction was as important as technical expertise.[14] During the 1950s and 1960s, others addressed the importance of communication between user and librarian. Robert S. Taylor's seminal article introducing the term *question negotiation* to describe the reference process was perhaps the most influential theoretical work of this period.[15] He proposed that there are "five filters through which a question passes, and from which the librarian selects significant data to aid him in his search."[16] These five filters were:

- determination of subject;
- objective and motivation;
- personal characteristics of inquirer;
- relationship of inquiry description to file organization;
- anticipated or acceptable answers.

Taylor's work influenced several related studies in the late 1960s and 1970s that emphasized the analysis and description of communication dynamics. Samuel Rothstein observed that these studies' "main achievement has been to make for greater awareness of the negotiation of the reference question as being in large part a communications problem."[17]

One of the most important components of this communication problem has often been users' inability to describe what they want to know. As Taylor put it:

> We are dealing here of course with a very subtle problem—how one person tries to find out what another person wants to know, when the latter cannot describe his need precisely.[18]

Some researchers believe that the users' inability to describe their need is experienced as an "anomalous state of knowledge" (ASK) involving a:

> somehow inadequate or incoherent state of knowledge . . . [where] an information need arises from a recognized anomaly in the user's state of knowledge concerning some topic or situation and that, in general, the user is unable to specify precisely what is needed to resolve that anomaly.[19]

Approaches to the Reference Process

Given the complexity of the reference encounter and the need to attend to its interpersonal dynamics, librarians have proposed a variety of approaches to the reference process. For example, Terry Ann Mood has claimed that the library profession is "embracing a 'new paradigm of reference.'"[20] In this paradigm—typified by the Brandeis University model—the librarian takes on the role of consultant.[21] Users make the first approach to paraprofessionals or graduate students who provide information desk service and refer users, as necessary, to the librarians, sometimes by appointment only. Others have suggested that the librarian should be viewed as a personal librarian[22] or a teacher.[23] Alternatively, Joan M. Bechtel suggested that the interaction be conceptualized as a conversation.[24] Elaine Z. Jennerich and Edward V. Jennerich's book, now in its second edition, views the reference encounter as a "creative art."[25]

Another approach applies psychological counseling techniques to reference.[26] Patrick R. Penland extensively studied the area of interviewing and advisory counseling. He advocated improved librarian–user communication through training in human relations and guidance counseling. Penland's book *Interpersonal Communication* integrated communication theory and research with library science, psychology, and mass communication.[27]

W. Bernard Lukenbill promoted utilization of the principles of the helping relationship as described by N. I. Brill in *Working with People: The Helping Process* that stressed the development of empathy, attentive behavior, and active listening.[28] Similarly, Pamela Tibbets proposed that librarians should have sensitivity training to "deal with the entire person and not just his information needs."[29] She argued that if librarians became more aware of users' needs and attitudes, they would serve those users better: "The librarian may find exactly what the person has asked for, but make him so miserable in the process that he will never come in again."[30] This presents a dilemma because the librarian wants to be held in high esteem as professionally and technically competent and yet strives to be viewed as approachable and nonthreatening. Eichman observed that many other professionals and nonprofessionals have to interact with individuals in ways similar to that of the librarian. One resemblance to other helping professions is that, in general, the user comes in person for assistance. The librarian must then gain the user's confidence and maintain it "long enough to provide the needed assistance."[31]

Several authors have compared librarianship to the medical profession and identified commonalities.[32] Carolyn J. Radcliff believes that librarian–user interactions can be "informed through the analysis of research into physician–patient relationships."[33] In the delivery of health care, the patient approaches the doctor with an illness that the doctor must diagnose and treat. "The patient is relatively unimportant in this process. The disease is of interest."[34] In the library setting, the user approaches with an information need that the librarian must diagnose and treat with available information-seeking methods, again implying, in this case, that the user is not important. Brenda Dervin believes that this "view of information and service does not work. Perhaps most obvious is the increasing demand by users of systems that they be treated as individuals."[35]

According to Marilyn D. White, however, the librarian–user relationship should be modeled on the interaction between doctor and patient. The diagnosis "is the mark of a truly professional encounter."[36] When patients come to the doctor, they may have already diagnosed the illness. The doctor, however, checks symptoms and makes his or her own diagnosis. Similarly, when the user approaches the reference librarian with a question (i.e., diagnosis), it is "still the librarian's professional responsibility to verify its accuracy."[37] White notes that many librarians are not comfortable with the role of diagnostician.

Studies of Librarians' Attitudes and Behaviors

Librarians' attitudes and behaviors play a central (if obvious) role in the success of the reference interaction. Anne V. Mathews studied the relationship between a librarian's self-acceptance and confirming behavior toward the user.[38] She identified four *confirming* behaviors:

- shows interest;

- replies appropriately;
- responds clearly;
- clarifies what has been said by a statement or rephrasing.

She also identified four *disconfirming* behaviors:

- shows indifference (does not look up from work);
- disqualifies user—type I (gives irrelevant, unclear, or contradictory reply);
- disqualifies user—type II (speaks for the other);
- demonstrates imperiousness (is critical of the other).

Other authors developed recommendations for improving and/or evaluating librarian–user interaction. A typical prescription was provided by White, who listed eleven indicators of rapport with and respect for users, among them:

- a positive, helpful attitude;
- absence of behavior that elicits defensiveness such as use of jargon, or a condescending or omniscient air;
- use of open questions when appropriate;
- sensitivity to client's frame of reference.[39]

Research has addressed some of White's points. For example, Brenda Dervin and Patricia Dewdney investigated the effects of "neutral questioning," a type of open-ended questioning.[40] This type of questioning is non-threatening to users as it avoids intruding upon them (e.g., asking why information is needed).

Mark V. Thompson, Nathan M. Smith, and Bonnie L. Woods proposed that appropriate librarian self-disclosure would help users to be more secure and comfortable.[41] Self-disclosure involves librarians giving users information about themselves such as admitting, "I am not sure where to look for this." Marilyn V. Markham, Keith H. Stirling, and Nathan M. Smith investigated the effect of librarian self-disclosure on user comfort and satisfaction levels. They found users to be more self-disclosing than librarians and recommended that "librarians cultivate and practice self-disclosure."[42]

Other scholars have identified reasons librarians may have difficulty with interpersonal aspects of reference. Geraldine B. King has argued that librarians have historically neglected interpersonal skills for two reasons:(1) they were not taught them in their professional courses; and (2) the literature on the reference encounter has been largely theoretical. Although some librarians have the natural ability to become excellent interviewers, the majority do not, King believes, and could vastly improve if given some basic training.[43] According to W. Bernard Lukenbill, library school faculty do not teach communication skills because they are not trained in the area.[44] Finally, Eichman points out that time constraints in reference interactions adversely affect communication. During busy times, when a daunting line of users forms at the reference desk, the librarian may only have a brief moment to devote to each user. These time constraints are not problematic in other interviewing situations such as the fifty minutes available to the psychotherapist or the carefully ordered appointment schedule of doctors and lawyers.[45]

The User's Perspective on the Reference Interaction

Recently, there has been a recognition of the importance of research that takes the user's point of view in study of the reference encounter.[46] For example, Patricia Dewdney and Catherine Ross reported on the experiences of seventy-seven MLS students who were directed to visit a library of their choice and ask a question that mattered to them. Only 59.7 percent reported they would be returning to the librarian with another question.[47] In another study, Susan Edwards and Mairead Browne took a user-based approach to see if clients and librarians differ in their expectations of quality information services. They found that "by-and-large there is a congruence between librarians and academics in what they view as characteristics of a quality information service." However, there are "points of departure between them" and librarians need to be made aware of these differences.[48]

This attention to the user's point of view may be a return to concerns of studies that were published in the 1970s. Howell, Reeves, and van Willigen examined the relative levels of satisfaction on the part of users versus librarians in reference encounters.[49] They found that librarians tended to rate their levels of performance less favorably than users. This finding suggested that librarians had much higher levels of expectation for their performance than did users. It also implied that users may not have been able to differentiate the quality of the information they received from their gratitude for being helped. Howell, Reeves and van Willigen proposed that "Questions aimed at discovering patron expectations for service and forcing patrons to make the distinction between the psychological and substantive outcome of reference encounters would be useful additions to future patron satisfaction survey instruments."[50] Finally, they found that users were more satisfied with the librarians if instruction was provided along with the information.[51]

A study by Helen Gothberg, published in the 1970s, applied the immediacy principle of communication scholar Albert Mehrabian to the reference process. The immediacy principle asserts that "people are drawn toward persons and things they like, evaluate highly, and prefer, and they avoid or move away from things they dislike, evaluate negatively, or do not prefer."[52] Gothberg found that users were more satisfied with the interview and with their own performance when the librarian had given them immediate verbal and/or nonverbal recognition. There was no difference in users' satisfaction with regard to the information received. These findings suggested "that a reference librarian who displays immediate verbal and nonverbal communication skills will engender in a user better feelings about himself and his experiences in the library."[53]

Nonverbal Communication

Nonverbal communication plays an important part in the success of reference encounters. Bissy Genova looked at intermediaries in presearch interviews. She sought to determine the nonverbal behaviors that facilitated or hindered the "smooth interaction flow of the interview," the correlation between these behaviors, and the satisfaction level of user and librarian.[54] Overall, Genova found that librarians were generally less satisfied than users. She also found that:

- When librarians used computer terminals, users were most satisfied.
- Librarians were less satisfied with long or interrupted interviews.

These findings indicated that interpersonal dimensions involving nonverbal communication entered into the process even when content-oriented thinking would say that the relevance of computer output (i.e., citations retrieved) should be the only factor to affect user and/or librarian satisfaction.

Gothberg's research also points to the important role of nonverbal communication in reference service.[55] The librarian usually sits behind a desk, available to users with questions. The decision to approach is made at the user's discretion before a word is spoken. Marie L. Radford found that users based their decisions on perceptions of nonverbal behavior.[56] Those librarians inviting the user to approach through exhibition of positive nonverbal behaviors (especially those making eye contact with users) were approached much more often than those exhibiting negative behaviors (such as looking down and busying themselves with paperwork).

Breaking Down Barriers between Users and Reference Librarians

Other researchers have studied users' reluctance to approach reference librarians. Mary Jane Swope and Jeffrey Katzer surveyed 199 people in an academic library and found that 32 (27%) had questions but would not ask a librarian for assistance.[57] The major reasons given were:

- dissatisfaction with previous librarian assistance;
- the belief that their query was too simple for the librarian;
- the disinclination to bother the librarian.

An incidental finding revealed that graduate students felt more pressure "not to appear stupid" than did undergraduates.[58]

Larason and Robinson discussed psychological cost as a barrier to communication. Psychological cost related to "the drain on an individual's self-concept, pride, or other mental/psychological attributes."[59] They described it as difficult to assess because it was often irrational (e.g., if a user needs help but avoids assistance that could provide this help because of psychological cost, it is a betrayal of self-interest). It may be that walking across the room to the reference desk to interact with a potentially condescending librarian could be too high a price to pay. Users may choose to try to find the information themselves, or even leave without it, rather than risk embarrassment.[60]

Librarians concerned with becoming more approachable have offered suggestions, not based on research, for evaluation and improvement of approachability and rapport with users.[61] For example, Ellis Mount's frequently cited "Communication Barriers and the Reference Question" stated that most library users ask questions that bear little resemblance to their true information need. He identified nine "invisible barriers to clear communication that often complicate giving of good reference service."[62] The barriers involve library users who:

- lack knowledge of the depth and quality of the collection;
- lack knowledge of the reference tools available;
- lack knowledge of the vocabulary used by a particular set of tools;
- do not willingly reveal reasons for needing information;
- have not decided what they really want;
- are not at ease in asking questions;

- feel that they cannot reveal the true question because of its sensitive nature;
- dislike reference staff members;
- lack confidence in the ability of the reference staff.

Effective reference requires that librarians bring down these barriers.

One general approach to improving users' receptivity to reference is to treat them as "customers." For example, Larason and Robinson compared the layout of the library to that of a department store and encouraged librarians to pay attention to packaging and marketing.[63] Christopher Millson-Martula and Vanaja Menon also believe that library users should be viewed as customers and that academic libraries should actively collect information about users through use of surveys, interviews, focus groups, and other assessment methods to "gain insight into their customer's needs" and to "play an active role in shaping user behavior and expectations."[64] Darlene E. Weingand's *Customer Service Excellence: A Concise Guide for Librarians* offers a wide range of advice on treating users as customers.[65]

Current Concerns

In addition to attention to variations on recurrent themes of information transfer and interpersonal factors, recent discussion of reference has addressed two increasingly important issues—the effects of information retrieval technology and the impact of increasing cultural diversity. Within the past ten years, there has been an astoundingly rapid proliferation of electronic information retrieval systems in academic libraries. Numerous articles have explored the impact of these systems and advances in telecommunications on the interactions between librarian and user and, on a broader level, on the future of reference itself.[66] Many authors wonder about the impact of these evolutionary (perhaps revolutionary) changes on the librarian's role. David W. Lewis noted that "Reference librarians need to see themselves as technology transfer agents, as the catalysts of the information revolution. They sit at the locus between students and faculty and the rapidly changing information technology.[67] He also warned that "those reference librarians who do not accept the challenge will be left behind."[68]

Anxiety, however, may be unwarranted. Technology, as Susan Anthes argued, calls for "high touch," or *increased* interpersonal involvement, between user and librarian as systems become more computerized and increasingly complex.[69] One reason for this is the increasing visibility of end-user systems, which have quickly become the norm in academic libraries. As contrasted to mediated search clients, end users require a different type of assistance that may involve increased expenditure of librarian attention, especially to first-time users and those with complex queries.[70]

Another growing area of concern focuses on our multicultural society. There has been an increase in ethnic diversity within the United States and in the number of foreign students in the country in recent years.[71] In interpersonal interactions with diverse populations, it is highly desirable to be aware of cultural differences and how they affect perceptions[72] and to be in touch with our own cultural bias.[73] There has also been recent attention given to differences in interpersonal communication patterns within American subcultures. R. Errol Lam, for example, discussed the need for better communication between African-American students and white librarians. He emphasized the importance of understanding the differences in both verbal and nonverbal communication styles.[74]

A Direction for Further Study of Librarian–User Interaction

Review of the literature shows that there has been considerable attention given to evaluation of reference service, most of which centers on measuring effectiveness in terms of getting the right answer. Ellsworth Mason and Jean Mason found that the literature on evaluation of accuracy in reference has overshadowed investigation of the perceptions of interpersonal communication in interactions.[75] Murfin and Gugelchuk commented that despite increasing publication about accuracy in reference, "substantial progress" is lacking.[76] Many observers agree that there needs to be more research from the user's point of view. Richard W. Budd stated that "the future of libraries and library studies relies heavily on the development of an overarching theory of information seeking and satiation. In short, it will demand intense focused research on users."[77]

As noted above, there have been studies that have centered on aspects of the interaction such as immediacy, questioning strategy, library anxiety, and librarian self-disclosure. But potentially fruitful approaches remain unexplored. J. W. Ellison has acknowledged the benefit of increased study of interpersonal communication theory and its application to librarianship.[78] Dervin has distinguished between the application of communication theory and the application of information theory to the study of user behavior in libraries. Information theory developed by Claude E. Shannon and Warren Weaver[79] "involves the quantitative study of signals sent from senders to receivers."[80] Dervin has argued that human communication and one's use of information is subjective in nature and not linear. Thus, communication theory, not information theory, is more important for librarianship.[81] Similarly, Stuart Glogoff has encouraged librarians to broaden their knowledge of communication theory in order to improve their understanding and promote more effective communication with users.[82]

Notes

1. Benita J. Howell, Edward B. Reeves, and John van Willigen, "Fleeting Encounters—A Role Analysis of Reference Librarian–Patron Interaction," *RQ* 16 (winter 1976): 125.

2. See Thompson R. Cummins, "Question Clarification in the Reference Encounter," *Canadian Library Journal* 41 (Apr. 1984): 63–67.

3. Samuel Rothstein, "Across the Desk: 100 Years of Reference Encounters," *Canadian Library Journal* 34 (1977): 397.

4. Wayne W. Crouch, *The Information Interview: A Comprehensive Bibliography and an Analysis of the Literature* (Washington D.C.: National Institute of Education [DHEW], 1979), 3. ERIC Document 180 501.

5. Heartsill Young, ed., *The ALA Glossary of Library and Information Science* (Chicago: ALA, 1983), 188.

6. Helen M. Gothberg, *Training Library Communication Skills: Development of 3 Video Tape Workshops* (Tuscon, Ariz.: Univ. of Arizona, 1977), 2. ERIC Document 163 934.

7. See Thomas Lee Eichman, "The Complex Nature of Opening Reference Questions," *RQ* 17 (1978): 212–22.

8. Marilyn Domas White, "Evaluation of the Reference Interview," *RQ* 25 (fall 1985): 77.

9. Studies of this type include: Frances Benham and Ronald R. Powell, *Success in Answering Reference Questions: Two Studies* (Metuchen, N.J.: Scarecrow, 1987); Vaughan P. Birbeck, "Unobtrusive Testing of Public Library Reference Service," *Refer* 4 (1986): 5–9; Thomas Childers, "The Quality of Reference: Still Moot after 20 Years," *Journal of Academic Librarianship* 13 (May 1987): 73–74; Ralph Gers and Lillie J. Seward, "Improving Reference Performance: Results of a Statewide Study," *Library Journal* 110 (Nov. 1985): 32–35; Charles R. McClure and Peter Hernon, *Improving the Quality of Reference Service for Government Publications* (Chicago: ALA, 1983); Marjorie E. Murfin and Gary M. Gugelchuk, "Development and Testing of a Reference Transaction Assessment Instrument, *College & Research Libraries* 48 (July 1987): 314. For an excellent overview of reference (and library) evaluation research, see Sharon L. Baker and Frederick W. Lancaster, *The Measure-*

ment and Evaluation of Library Services. 2nd ed. (Arlington, Va.: Information Resources Pr., 1991).

10. Fredrick Wilfrid Lancaster, *If You Want to Evaluate Your Library . . .* (Champaign, Illinois.: Univ. of Ill. Pr., 1988), 113.

11. See Peter Hernon and Charles R. McClure, "Library Reference Service: An Unrecognized Crisis—A Symposium," *Journal of Academic Librarianship* 13 (May 1987): 69–80.

12. "Guidelines for Behavioral Performance of Reference and Information Services Professionals," *RQ* 36 (winter 1996): 200.

13. For criticism of research on the 55% Rule, see: William G. Bailey, "The '55 Percent Rule' Revisited," *Journal of Academic Librarianship* 13 (Nov. 1987): 280–82; Joan C. Durrance, "Reference Success: Does the 55 Percent Rule Tell the Whole Story?" *Library Journal* 119 (Apr. 1989): 31–36; Carol C. Kuhlthau, *Seeking Meaning: A Process Approach to Library and Information Services* (Norwood, N.Y.: Ablex, 1993); Murfin and Gugelchuk, "Development and Testing;" David Shavit, "Qualitative Evaluation of Reference Service," *Reference Librarian* 11 (fall/winter 1984): 237–38; Jo Bell Whitlatch, "Reference Service Effectiveness," *RQ* 30 (winter 1990): 213.

14. Margaret Hutchins, *Introduction to Reference Work* (Chicago: ALA, 1944).

15. Robert S. Taylor, "Question Negotiation and Information Seeking in Libraries," *College & Research Libraries* 29 (May 1968): 178–94.

16. Ibid., 183.

17. Rothstein, "Across the Desk," 395.

18. Taylor, "Question Negotiation and Information Seeking in Libraries" 179.

19. Nicholas J. Belkin, Robert N. Oddy, and Helen M. Brooks, "ASK for Information Retrieval, Part I: Background and Theory," *Journal of Documentation* 38 (June 1982): 62, 64.

20. Terry Ann Mood, "Of Sundials and Digital Watches: A Further Step toward the New Paradigm of Reference," *Reference Services Review* 22 (fall 1994): 27–32, 95.

21. Virginia Massey-Burzio, "Reference Encounters of a Different Kind: A Symposium," *Journal of Academic Librarianship* 18 (Nov. 1992): 276.

22. Bill Bailey, "The Personal Librarian," *Library Journal* 109 (1984): 1820–21.

23. Brian Nielsen, "Teacher or Intermediary: Alternative Professional Models in the Information Age," *College & Research Libraries* 43 (May 1982): 183–91; and Jane Rice, "Library-Use Instruction with Individual Users: Should Instruction be Included in the Reference Interview," *Reference Librarian* 10 (spring/summer 1984): 75–84.

24. Joan M. Bechtel, "Conversation: A New Paradigm for Librarianship?" *College & Research Libraries* 47 (May 1986): 219–24.

25. Elaine Z. Jennerich and Edward J. Jennerich, *The Reference Interview as a Creative Art*, 2nd ed. (Englewood, Colo.: Libraries Unlimited, 1997).

26. See, for example, Milena Awaritefe, "Psychology Applied to Librarianship," *International Library Review* 16 (Jan. 1984): 27–33; Barbara L. Stein, James D.

Hand, and Herman L. Totten, "Understanding Preferred Cognitive Styles—A Tool for Facilitating Better Communication," *Journal of Education for Library and Information Science* 27 (summer 1986): 38–49.

27. Patrick R. Penland, *Interpersonal Communication: Counseling, Guidance, and Retrieval for Media, Library, and Information Specialists* (New York: Dekker, 1974); see also Theodore P. Peck, "Counseling Skills Applied to Reference Services," *RQ* 14 (spring 1975): 233–35.

28. See W. Bernard, Lukenbill, "Teaching Helping Relationship Concepts in the Reference Process," *Journal of Education for Librarianship* 18 (fall 1977): 110–20.

29. Pamela Tibbetts, "Sensitivity Training—A Possible Application for Librarianship," *Special Libraries* 65 (Dec. 1974): 494.

30. Ibid., 494.

31. Eichman, "The Complex Nature of Opening Reference Questions," 212.

32. Rachael Naismith, "Reference Communication: Commonalities in the Worlds of Medicine and Librarianship," *College & Research Libraries* 57 (Jan. 1996): 44–57.

33. Carolyn J. Radcliff, "Interpersonal Communication with Library Patrons: Physician–Patient Research Models," *RQ* 34 (summer 1995): 497.

34. Brenda Dervin, "Useful Theory for Librarianship: Communication, Not Information," *Drexel Library Quarterly* 13 (July 1977): 18.

35. Ibid., 18.

36. White, "Evaluation of the Reference Interview," 77.

37. Ibid., 77.

38. Anne J. Mathews, "Confirming and Disconfirming Behaviors, Self Acceptance and Personal Values: A Descriptive Study of Librarian–User Interactions." (Ph.D. diss., Univ. of Denver, 1977).

39. White, "Evaluation of the Reference Interview."

40. Brenda Dervin and Patricia Dewdney, "Neutral Questioning: A New Approach to the Reference Interview," *RQ* 25 (summer 1986): 506–13.

41. Mark J. Thompson, Nathan M. Smith, and Bonnie L. Woods, "A Proposed Model of Self-Disclosure," *RQ* 20 (winter 1980): 160–64.

42. Marilyn J. Markham, Keith H. Stirling, and Nathan M. Smith, "Librarian Self-Disclosure and Patron Satisfaction in the Reference Interview," *RQ* 22 (summer 1983): 373.

43. Geraldine B. King, "The Reference Interview," *RQ* 12 (1972); see also Patricia Dewdney, "The Effects of Training Reference Librarians in Interview Skills: A Field Experiment" (Ph.D. diss., School of Library and Information Service, Univ. of Western Ontario, 1987).

44. Lukenbill, "Teaching Helping Relationship Concepts in the Reference Process."

45. Eichman, "The Complex Nature of Opening Reference Questions,"

46. See, for example, Ruth C. T. Morris, "Toward a User-Centered Information Service," *Journal of the American Society for Information Science* 45 (Jan. 1994): 20–30.

47. Patricia Dewdney and Catherine Sheldrick Ross, "Flying a Light Aircraft: Reference Service Evaluation from the user's viewpoint," *RQ 34* (winter 1994): 224.

48. Susan Edwards and Mairead Browne, "Quality in Information Services: Do Users and Librarians Differ in Their Expectations?" *Library and Information Science Research* 17 (spring 1995): 181.

49. Howell, Reeves, and van Willigen, "Fleeting Encounters."

50. Ibid., 127.

51. Ibid., 127.

52. Albert Mehrabian. *Silent Messages* (Belmont, Calif.: Wadsworth, 1971), 1.

53. Helen M. Gothberg, "Immediacy: A Study of Communication Effect of the Reference Process," *Journal of Academic Librarianship* 2 (July 1976): 129.

54. Bissy Genova, *Nonverbal Behaviors in Presearch Interviews* (Bethesda, Md.: National Library of Medicine [DHEW], 1981), viii. ERIC Document 205 188.

55.See also the following articles on nonverbal behavior and librarians: Virginia Boucher, "Nonverbal Communication and the Library Reference Interview," *RQ* 16 (fall 1976): 27–32; Marynelle DeVore-Chew, Brian Roberts, and Nathan M. Smith, "The Effects of Reference Librarians' Nonverbal Communications on the Patrons' Perceptions of the Library, Librarians, and Themselves," *Library and Information Science Research* 10 (Oct./Dec. 1988): 389–400; John W. Ellsion, "How Approachable Are You as a Public Service Librarian?" *Unabashed Librarian* 46 (1983): 4–6; Stuart Glogoff, "Communication Theory's Role in the Reference Interview," *Drexel Library Quarterly* 19 (spring 1983): 56–72; Richard Heinzkill, "Introducing Nonverbal Communication," *RQ* 11 (summer 1972): 356–58; Edward Kazlauskas, "An Exploratory Study: A Kinesic Analysis of Academic Library Public Service Points," *Journal of Academic Librarianship* 2 (July 1976): 130–34; Larry Larason and Judith Schiek Robinson, "The Reference Desk: Service Point or Barrier?" *RQ* 23 (spring 1984): 332–38; Joanna L. Munoz, "The Significance of Nonverbal Communication in the Reference Interview," *RQ* 16 (spring 1977): 220–24; Joanna Richardson, "Evaluating Nonverbal Behaviour in the Reference Interview," *International Library Movement* 7 (1985): 117–23; Kay Weiss, *The Impact of Nonverbal Communications on the Public Services Functions of Libraries* (Washington, D.C.: National Institute of Education [DHEW], 1976). ERIC Document 153 659; Marie L. Radford, "Interpersonal Communication Theory in the Library Context: A Review of Current Perspectives," in *Library and Information Science Annual*, ed. Bohdan S. Wynar. Vol. 5, pp. 3–10 (Englewood, Colo.: Libraries Unlimited, 1989).

56. Marie L. Radford, "A Qualitative Investigation of Nonverbal Immediacy in the User's Decision to Approach the Academic Reference Librarian," presented at the Library Research Seminar I, Florida State University, Tallahassee, Fla., Nov. 1–2, 1996.

57. Mary Jane Swope and Jeffrey Katzer, "Why Don't They Ask Questions?" *RQ* 12 (winter 1972): 161–66.

58. Ibid., 164. Mengxiong Liu and Bernice Redfern, "Information-Seeking Behavior of Multicultural Students: A Case Study at San Jose State University,"

College & Research Libraries 58 (July 1997): 348–54, had a similar finding in a study of multicultural students who were also reluctant to "bother the librarian" when they needed help.

59. Larason and Robinson, "The Reference Desk," 333.

60. See also Erving Goffman, *The Presentation of Self in Everyday Life* (Garden City, N.Y.: Doubleday Anchor, 1959); ———, *Behavior in Public Places* (New York: Free Pr., 1963); ———, *Interaction Ritual, Essays on Face-to-Face Behavior* (Garden City, N.Y.; Anchor, 1967); ———, *Relations in Public: Microstudies of the Public Order* (New York: Basic Bks., 1971); ———, *Forms of Talk* (Philadelphia: Univ. of Pennsylvania Pr., 1981).

61. For example, see Charles A. Bunge, "Interpersonal Dimensions of the Reference Interview: A Historical Review of the Literature," *Drexil Library Quarterly* 20 (spring 1984): 4–23; Barron Holland, "Updating Library Reference Services through Training for Interpersonal Competence," *RQ* 17 (spring 1978): 207–11; William F. Young, "Methods for Evaluating Reference Desk Performance," *RQ* 25 (fall 1985): 69–75.

62. Ellis Mount, "Communication Barriers and the Reference Question," *Special Libraries* 57 (Oct. 1966): 575.

63. Larason and Robinson, "Reference Desk," 336.

64. Christopher Millson-Martula and Vanaja Menon, "Customer Expectations: Concepts and Reality for Academic Library Services," *College & Research Libraries* 56 (Jan. 1995): 36.

65. Darlene E. Weingand, *Customer Service Excellence: A Concise Guide for Librarians* (Chicago: ALA, 1997). See also Joanne M. Bessler, *Putting Service into Library Staff Training* (Chicago: ALA, 1994); John H. Sandy, "By Any Other Name, They're Still Our Customers," *American Libraries* 28 (Aug. 1997): 43–45; Suzanne Walters, *Customer Service: A How-to-Do-It Manual for Librarians* (New York: Neal-Schuman Publishers, 1994). For a critique of conceiving users as customers, see John M. Budd, "A Critique of Customer and Commodity," *College & Research Libraries* 58 (July 1997): 319.

66. For example, see Toni Carbo Bearman, ed., "Educating the Future Information Professional," *Library-Hi-Tech* 5 (summer 1987): 27–40; William Katz, *Introduction to Reference Work,* 7th ed. (New York: McGraw Hill, 1997); Harry M. Kibirige, "Computer-Assisted Reference Services: What the Computer Will Not Do," *RQ* 27 (spring 1988): 377–83; Brian Nielsen and Betsy Baker, "Educating the Online Catalog User: A Model Evaluation Study," *Library Trends* 35 (spring 1987): 571–85; Carol Tenopir, "Online Databases: Costs and Benefits of CD-ROM," *Library Journal* 112 (Sept. 1987): 156–57.

67. David W. Lewis, "Making Academic Reference Services Work," *College & Research Libraries* 55 (Sept. 1994): 454.

68. Ibid., 454. See also John C. Stalker and Marjorie E. Murfin, "Why Reference Librarians Won't Disappear: A Study of Success in Identifying Answering Sources for Reference Questions," *RQ* 35 (summer 1996): 489–503.

69. Susan H. Anthes, "High Tech/High Touch; Academic Libraries Respond to Change in the Behavioral Sciences," *Behavioral & Social Sciences Librarian* 5 (fall 1985): 53–65.

70. See Geraldene Walker and Joseph Janes, *Online Retrieval: A Dialog of Theory and Practice* (Englewood, Colo.: Libraries Unlimited, 1993).

71. Liu and Redfern, "Information-Seeking Behavior of Multicultural Students," Irene Hoffman and Opritsa Popa, "Library Orientation and Instruction for International Students: The University of California-Davis Experience," *RQ* 25 (spring 1986): 356–60.

72. See Kwasi Sarkodie-Mensah, "Dealing with International Students in a Multicultural Era," *Journal of Academic Librarianship* 18 (Sept. 1992): 214–16.

73. Patrick A. Hall, "Peanuts: A Note on Intercultural Communication," *Journal of Academic Librarianship* 18 (Sept. 1992): 211. For additional articles addressing this concern within the library setting, see: Louise Greenfield, Susan Johnston, and Karen Williams, "Educating the World: Training Library Staff to Communicate Effectively with International Students," *Journal of Academic Librarianship* 12 (Sept. 1986): 227–31; Terry Ann Mood, "Foreign Students and the Academic Library," *RQ* 22 (winter 1982): 175–80; Sally G. Wayman, "The International Student in the Academic Library," *Journal of Academic Librarianship* 9 (Jan. 1984): 336–41.

74. R. Errol Lam, "The Reference Interview: Some Intercultural Considerations," *RQ* 27 (spring 1988): 390–95.

75. Ellsworth Mason and Jean Mason, "The Whole Shebang—Comprehensive Evaluation of Reference Operations, " *Reference Librarian* 11 (fall/winter 1984): 26.

76. Murfin and Gugelchuk, "Development and Testing of a Reference Transaction Assessment Instrument," 315.

77. Richard W. Budd, "Review of *The Measurement and Evaluation of Library Service* by Sharon L. Baker and F. Wilfrid Lancaster," *Library Quarterly* 62 (Oct. 1992): 461.

78. J. W. Ellison, "How Approachable Are You as a Public Service Librarian?" *Unabashed Librarian* 46 (1983): 4.

79. Claude E. Shannon, and Warren Weaver, *The Mathematical Theory of Communication* (Urbana, Ill.: Univ. of Illinois Pr., 1949).

80. Stephen J. Littlejohn, *Theories of Human Communication,* 5th ed. (Belmont, Calif.: Wadsworth, 1996), 52.

81. Dervin, "Useful Theory for Librarianship."

82. Glogoff, "Communication Theory's Role in the Reference Interview."

Chapter 3

Communication Theory and the Reference Interaction

❧❧ ❧❧ ❧❧ ❧❧ ❧❧ ❧❧ ❧❧ ❧❧ ❧❧

*I*nterpersonal communication, or communication between persons, is a fundamental part of the work performed by librarians within the reference process. Librarians can learn much from scholars of communication. For example, consider rapport building, which involves conversation encouraging give and take, establishment of mutual understanding, and development of relationships. A reference librarian in an academic library was once asked: "Where are the *Psychological Abstracts* located?" She in turn asked: "Have you ever used them before?" Receiving a hesitant shake of the head in reply, the librarian then launched into a description of the organization and use of this index. The student interrupted to explain impatiently that she needed the location of *Psychological Abstracts* in order to meet one of her professors in front of them.[1]

Although this may seem to be merely a simple "misunderstanding," it is a good example of how even an apparently uncomplicated query can be misconstrued. The librarian "read into" the location question, did not take it literally as intended but, instead, assumed that the user would want to proceed to use the index, as is the case in the usual reference scenario. This student merely needed to know the location; therefore, any other information was superfluous. In more complex question negotiations, in which the user may not have a clear idea of the information he or she seeks, the chances of miscommunication and misunderstanding are even more greatly increased. If the librarian had not blithely launched into an explanation of how *Psycho-*

logical Abstracts was used but, instead, had taken a moment to develop rapport—to ask the user if she was interested in learning about its use—the miscommunication could easily have been avoided. A brief conversational exchange that enabled librarian and user to understand one another could have prevented this moment of embarrassment and frustration.

In drawing upon communication theory to analyze and understand situations such as this, it is important to note that communication theory does not refer to any single theory or even a single object of study. Rather, it "can be used to designate the collective wisdom found in the entire body of theories related to the communication process."[2] Seminal theories of communication developed between the late 1940s and the 1960s embraced a linear design in which messages and information are transmitted from a source to a receiver.[3] Communication is conceptualized as unidirectional and linear with the content (informational) aspect of a message being of primary importance.[4] The linear model's emphasis on unidirectional transfer of content parallels the emphasis in the library profession that characterizes the reference interaction as transfer of information from the librarian to the user. In the example above, the librarian has information (how to use *Psychological Abstracts*) that needs to be delivered to the open and waiting mind of the user. Librarians frequently operate on this premise and then are very surprised to find out that the user may have another purpose and a different interpretation of the reference interaction.

In contrast to the content-centered conceptualizations of communication, a group of theories making up the relational view of communication favors a process model that characterizes communication as ongoing, dynamic, and reflexive, as opposed to static and linear. The relational view applies the premises of systems theory to human communication and the ideas of psychologists Jurgen Reusch and Gregory Bateson.[5]

Systems theory was developed by Ludwig von Bertalanffy who believed that the world should be thought of as being composed of wholes and interrelated parts.[6] Systems theory aims to "integrate accumulated knowledge into a clear and realistic framework" and emphasizes the relationships between system members.[7] A *system* can be defined as "a set of objects together with relationships between the objects and between their attributes."[8] According to Stephen J. Littlejohn, a system has four components:

1. objects or members;
2. attributes, qualities, or properties;
3. relationships among objects;
4. the environment.[9]

From a systems perspective, control over the communication process is shared among the members of the interpersonal system rather than held in the hands of the sender (as assumed in the linear model). Also from the standpoint of systems theory:

> human communication is not a one-way process, as suggested by sender-message-channel-receiver oriented models . . . but rather a multidirectional phenomenon with no distinguishable beginning or end.[10]

The premises of systems theorists were key to the development of the relational model of communication by a group of researchers that included Bateson, Watzlawick, Beavin, and Jackson. They worked together at the Mental Research Institute in Palo Alto, California, and became known as the Palo Alto Group, or the pragmatists. These researchers conceptualized the communication process as an open system.[11] Because open systems interact with the environment, they saw the context of a communication act as highly important. "Environments characteristically affect the systems which interact with them and are, in turn, affected by those systems."[12] As an interpersonal system changes in response to the environment or to changes within system members, the context of the message changes. In the systems view, there is no fixed meaning for a message. Messages are given meaning from the context in which they exist.

The now-classic *Pragmatics of Human Communication* provides the foundation for a large body of interpersonal communication research.[13] It deals with "pragmatic (behavioral) effects of communication" and identifies simple properties or "axioms" of human interaction. The key proposed axiom is: "Every communication has a content and a relationship aspect such that the latter classifies the former and is therefore a metacommunication."[14] Thus, every communication has dual dimensions: content/report and relationship/command. To clarify these concepts, "The report aspect conveys information and is, therefore, synonymous in human communication with the *content* of the message,"[15] whereas "The command aspect, on the other hand, refers to what sort of a message it is to be taken as, and, therefore, ultimately to the *relationship* between the communicants."[16] F. E. Millar and L. Edna Rogers interpret content as referring to "the object or referent specified in the message," whereas relational characteristics refer to the "reciprocal rules of interdependence that combine the persons into an interactive system."[17]

It is important to understand that the relational model proposed by the pragmatists is concerned with both the effect of communication on the receiver and the effect the receiver's reaction has on the sender. Thus, focus is on "the sender–receiver relation, as mediated by communication."[18] The interactivity of the communication process is of vital importance to the pragmatists who reject theories that "limit themselves to the study of communication as a one-way phenomenon (from speaker to listener) and stop short of looking at communication as an *interaction* process."[19]

One of the assumptions of a linear model is that the sender (or source) of a message is in control, that the goal of communication is to transfer information from sender to receiver.[20] The relational perspective asserts that control is not centered in the sender nor in the receiver, rather, they are both part of a larger system that forms their relationship.

Additional axioms proposed by Watzlawick and his colleagues describe other important aspects of communication. One proposes that "human beings communicate both digitally and analogically."[21] Digital code is verbal language; analogic code is nonverbal.[22] Another axiom distinguishes symmetrical and complementary interactions.[23]

When two communicators in a relationship behave similarly, the relationship is said to be symmetrical; differences are minimized. When communicator differences are maximized, however, a complementary relationship is said to exist.[24]

Following from this, the librarian–user interaction would be conceptualized as a complementary relationship because there is a difference in power, control, and status:

> A boss–employee relationship is usually complementary, as are those between teacher–student, doctor–patient, policeman–automobile driver, president–secretary and other relationships based on inequality of control.[25]

Value of the Pragmatic/Relational Perspective

The field of communication has many different theoretical approaches yet lacks a general, unified idea.[26] B. Aubrey Fisher points out that:

> every theory of communication is another level of communication—a metacommunication—and is itself a created reality. The pragmatic perspective of human communication is certainly no exception.[27]

Although the relational perspective of the pragmatists is a "created reality," and not without its critics,[28] librarians have much to gain by an examination of this work and its implications for the reference interaction. One major implication is that in order to fully understand the communication process and to construct theory that is an accurate representation or model, it is vital to view communication as a dynamic and interactive process rather than as linear or static. Both the content of a message and its metacommunication (i.e., communication *about* communication) characteristics must be taken into account because both are integral parts of the process. In reference interactions, this implies that focusing exclusively on the exchange of information, of finding the "right answer" to a user's query, discounts the importance of the interpersonal dimensions. Yes, users may be given the correct information, but if they are embarrassed or made to feel uncomfortable in the process, a successful information exchange can be interpreted by the user as unsuccessful. Thus, human communication does not merely exist on the content level. Rather, it exists as part of an interactive system, taking place between the source and receiver. It is, therefore, not appropriate to study instances of communication removed from the context in which they occur. In the reference interaction, output measures (such as counts of reference transactions) may be provided as sole evidence of reference effectiveness. According to relational models, reporting reference statistics can give evidence of activity but alone can not be used as evidence of effectiveness.

As part of a system, messages do not have fixed meaning and may change over time as a relationship changes. It is also inappropriate to minimize or discount the impact that feedback has on the relational system. As a communication interaction unfolds, feedback promotes constant motion and change in the system's structure. This implies that reference service can be better evaluated by asking users for feedback, formally through surveys or interviews, or informally at the reference desk. User feedback can then be used to promote positive changes in reference service.[29]

Another implication of the pragmatic approach is that "Content competence is not equal to relational competence."[30] This is particularly important to the problems of the librarian–user interaction. As noted in chapter 2, many studies have defined competence as being related to the search for the "right" answer. If evaluations of reference personnel consider "efficiency" and "effectiveness" to be the only indicators of competence, librarians who find the right answer may be regarded as competent even though their relational abilities, or "people skills," are lacking.

Implications of Communication Literature for Study of Librarian–User Interaction

The review of communication literature suggests several implications for study of librarian–user interactions. As noted in chapter 2, there are many gaps in the research regarding the interpersonal relationship between librarian and user. In particular, limited attention has been paid to the user's perspective. From the pragmatic point of view, this has been a critical oversight. As a full-fledged member of the interpersonal communication system, the user is more than a passive vessel waiting to be filled with information.

Another, related major implication is that the librarian–user interaction can no longer be viewed as a linear process. Instead, the encounter between librarian and user must be conceived as a process of interaction between the two. Communication theory offers approaches such as the relational model of the pragmatists and impression management that allow focus on the user and the relationship-building aspect of library encounters.[31]

Library researchers have begun to realize that the relational, interpersonal aspects of the librarian–user interaction are vitally important. Their work has found that attention to relational characteristics (such as self-disclosure, immediacy, and nonverbal approachability) leads to increased user satisfaction and comfort in the interaction. There is further need for research in this area that includes both content and relational dimensions, provides both librarian and user perspectives, and recognizes the importance of context provided by study in a naturalistic setting. These needs and the above theoretical foundations have shaped the study design and methodology reported in this book.

Notes

1. This example was also used in Marie L. Radford, "Interpersonal Communication Theory in the Library Context: A Review of Current Perspectives," in *Library and Information Science Annual*, ed. Bohdan S. Wynar. Vol. 5, pp. 3–10 (Englewood, Colo.: Libraries Unlimited, 1989).

2. Stephen J. Littlejohn, *Theories of Human Communication*, 5th ed. (Belmont, Calif.: Wadsworth, 1996), 3.

3. For example, Claude E. Shannon and Warren Weaver, *The Mathematical Theory of Communication* (Urbana, Ill.: Univ. of Ill. Pr., 1949); Norbert Wiener, *Cybernetics, or Control and Communication in the Animal and the Machine* (Cambridge, Mass.: Technology Pr., 1948); David K. Berlo, *The Process of Communication* (New York: Holt, 1960).

4. Nancy Harper, *Human Communication Theory: The History of a Paradigm* (Rochelle Park, N.J.: Hayden, 1979).

5. Jurgen Ruesch and Gregory Bateson *Communication: The Social Matrix of Psychiatry* (New York: Norton, 1951).

6. Ludwig von Bertalanffy, "General Systems Theory: A Critical Review," *General Systems* 7 (1962): 1–20; ———, *General Systems Theory, Foundations, Developments, Applications* (New York: Braziller, 1968). For more in-depth discussions of systems theory, see Littlejohn, *Theories of Human Communication*; Peter R. Monge, "The Systems Perspective as a Theoretical Basis for the Study of Human Communication," *Communication Quarterly* 25 (winter 1977): 19–29; Brent D. Ruben and John Y. Kim, *General Systems Theory and Human Communication*, (Rochelle Park, N.J.: Hayden, 1975).

7. Littlejohn, *Theories of Human Communication*, 2nd ed., 1983, 37.

8. A. D. Hall and R. E. Fagen, "Definition of System," in *General Systems Theory and Human Communication*, ed. Brent D. Ruben and John Y. Kim (Rochelle Park, N.J.: Hayden 1975), 52.

9. Littlejohn, *Theories of Human Communication*, 1996.

10. Brent D. Ruben, "General Systems Theory," in *Interdisciplinary Approaches to Human Communication*, ed. Richard W. Budd and Brent D. Ruben, (Rochelle Park, N.J.: Hayden, 1979), 120.

11. See Monge, "The Systems Perspective as a Theoretical Basis for the Study of Human Communication," 1977.

12. Ruben, "General Systems Theory," 126.

13. Paul Watzlawick, Janet Helmick Beavin, and Don J. Jackson, *Pragmatics of Human Communication: A Study of Interactional Patterns, Pathologies, and Paradoxes* (New York: Norton, 1967). For examples of the application of relational theory, see Judee K. Burgoon, David B. Buller, and W. Gill Woodall, *Nonverbal Communication: The Unspoken Dialogue* (New York: Harper & Row, 1989); Judee K. Burgoon and Jerold L. Hale, "The Fundamental Topoi of Relational Communication," *Communication Monographs* 51 (Sept. 1984): 193–214; B. Aubrey Fisher and Katherine L. Adams, *Interpersonal Communication: Pragmatics of Human Relationships*, 2nd ed. (New York: McGraw-Hill, 1994); Littlejohn, *Theories of Human*

Communication, 1996; Robert Martin, "Relational Cognition Complexity and Relational Communication in Personal Relationships," *Communication Monographs* 59 (June 1992): 150–63; Frank E. Millar and L. Edna Rogers, "A Relational Approach to Interpersonal Communication," in *Explorations in Interpersonal Communication,* ed. Gerald R. Miller (Beverly Hills, Calif.: Sage, 1976), 87–104; William W. Wilmot, *Relational Communication* 4th ed. (New York: McGraw-Hill, 1995); Julia T. Wood, *Relational Communication: Continuity and Change in Personal Relationships* (Belmont, Calif.: Wadsworth, 1995).

14. Watzlawick et al, *Pragmatics of Human Communication,"* 54.

15. Ibid., 51.

16. Ibid., 52.

17. Millar and Rogers "A Relational Approach to Interpersonal Communication," 87. For additional explanations of these concepts, see Fisher and Adams, *Interpersonal Communication,* 1994; B. Aubrey Fisher, "The Pragmatic Perspective of Human Communication: A View from System Theory," in *Human Communication Theory: Comparative Essays,* ed. Francis E. X. Dance (New York: Harper & Row, 1982),192–219; Littlejohn, *Theories of Human Communication,* 1996; Malcom R. Parks, "Relational Communication: Theory and Research," *Human Communication Research* 3 (summer 1977): 372–81.

18. Watzlawick, et al, *Pragmatics of Human Communication,* 22.

19. Ibid., 14.

20. Brent D. Ruben, *Communication and Human Behavior,* 2nd ed. (New York: Macmillan, 1988).

21. Watzlawick et al., *Pragmatics of Human Communication,* 67.

22. Littlejohn, *Theories of Human Communication,* 1996.

23. Watzlawick et al., *Pragmatics of Human Communication.*

24. Littlejohn, *Theories of Human Communication,* 3rd ed. 1989, 177.

25. William W. Wilmot, *Dyadic Communication,* 2nd ed. (New York: Random House, 1980), 102.

26. Littlejohn, *Theories of Human Communication,* 1996.

27. Fisher, *The Pragmatic Perspective of Human Communication,* 216.

28. See Littlejohn, *Theories of Human Communication,* 1996.

29. See Suzanne Walters, *Customer Service: A How-to-Do-It Manual For Librarians.* (New York: Neal-Schuman Publishers, 1994); Darlene E. Weingand, *Customer Service Excellence: A Concise Guide for Librarians* (Chicago: ALA, 1997).

30. Wilmot, *Dyadic Communication,* 98.

31. See Mary Kathleen Chelton, "Adult–Adolescent Service Encounters: The Library Context" (Ph.D. diss., Rutgers—State Univ. of New Jersey, 1997), for a doctoral dissertation that applies Goffman's impression management to the study of adult–adolescent interaction in libraries.

Chapter 4

Methodology

ꙮ ꙮ ꙮ ꙮ ꙮ ꙮ ꙮ ꙮ ꙮ

*T*his chapter describes the selection of sites, subjects, and procedures and methodology used in data collection and analysis for a pilot study and the main study.

Pilot Study

The first phase of the research design consisted of a pilot study conducted at a state-supported college in the Northeast.[1] For the pilot study, the author interviewed two academic reference librarians[2] and three academic library users.[3] There were two goals: (1) to refine design and methodology, and (2) to develop a framework for analysis.

The interviews consisted of open-ended questions structured on the research questions (see chapter 1). General topics covered in the interviews included: successful and unsuccessful reference interviews; desirable and undesirable characteristics of users and librarians; and factors that impact these. In addition, there were questions using the critical incident technique.[4] The critical incident technique, (described below) involves asking librarians and users to recall and describe positive and negative interactions. Interview questions were used as guides and were modified as appropriate to the context of the interview.

The author transcribed the tape recordings of the five pilot interviews verbatim. She then identified and categorized issues or themes discussed by the librarians and users (see below for an explanation of the development of the outline of categories), and analyzed the pilot interview data using the critical incident technique.

Summary of Pilot Study Contributions

Using the information obtained in the pilot study, the author developed a preliminary outline of categories.[5] Three major categories (or themes) emerged :

- goals or aims of the interaction;
- facilitators: qualities that enhance goals, communication;
- barriers: characteristics that impede goals, communication.

These categories are discussed further in chapter 5. Together with the critical incident analysis, they provided an emerging model of librarian and user perceptions of their interaction and the necessary framework for further analysis.[6]

The pilot also helped to refine the design of the main study in several ways. Methodology was greatly enhanced, for example, by using the preliminary outline of categories to develop a coding scheme for analysis of the critical incidents. Results confirmed that individual interviews would enable the author to collect data to inform the research questions. In addition, the author developed her interviewing technique, modified the content of the interview questions, and adjusted the wording and order of some questions and dropped others. She also improved the other data collection instruments based on findings from the pilot study.

Main Study

Building on the results of the pilot study, the methodology of the main study was expanded to include an additional analysis involving observation and interviews of librarian–user pairs interacting in reference encounters. The author recorded in-depth interviews with nine academic reference librarians and twenty-nine users. In addition, she studied librarian and user perceptions of the same twenty-seven specific reference interactions to determine the role of the relational dimensions of communication. The author interviewed the librarian–user pairs immediately after they interacted. This allowed for a comparison of the librarian's and user's perceptions of the same interaction. It also enabled the author to analyze:

- user perceptions of interactions;
- librarian perceptions of interactions;
- comparison of librarian and user perceptions of the same interactions.

The researcher considered twenty-seven interactions numerous enough to provide confidence in the results.[7] This number allowed her to collect data from the selected sites at varying times of the day, days of the week, and over the course of the semester.[8]

Selection and Description of Sites

The author chose three types of academic libraries in the Northeast as research sites: a public community college, a private university, and a public college. These types of institutions differ in the number and levels of degrees offered, levels of sophistication of the students, and purpose or mission. The author selected these institutions to provide a wide range of types of users and librarians within the academic library population.

Site A is a public community college offering associate's degrees. It has approximately 10,500 students from low to middle class and is located in a rural area. Its varied student body is composed of many nontraditional and vocational students with a wide range of academic abilities, the majority being average.

Site B is a private university. It has a small, affluent population of approximately 2,200 students and is situated in a culturally rich suburban area. It offers bachelor's, master's, and doctoral degrees, and accepts students with above–average academic ability.

Site C is a public college. It has approximately 13,000 students, largely from the middle class, and is located in an urban area. Its racially and culturally diverse student population has a wide range of academic abilities, the majority being average. It offers bachelor's and master's degrees, with 80 percent of the students enrolled in undergraduate programs.

Subjects
Librarians

The researcher recruited three reference librarians from each of the three sites to participate in the study. In asking for volunteers, she only revealed that the study focused on information-seeking behavior during the reference interview. She also informed the participants that they would be observed and interviewed and that the purpose of the research was not to evaluate their professional performance or abilities but, rather, to understand the dynamics of information-seeking behavior. The informants were therefore self-selected, yet were not told the exact nature of the study so that bias would be kept to a minimum.

The researcher gathered demographic information on the education, background, and reference experience of the librarians who participated in the study.[9] The nine librarians included two males and seven females. Six of them were willing to give their age, which ranged from thirty-one to fifty seven years with a mean of forty-one. All nine held a master's degree in library science and three held a second master's degree, each in a different subject field. Two were full-time academic reference librarians, and the remaining seven were part-time reference librarians with a variety of full- or part-time responsibilities in other library positions.

The amount of time the librarians interacted with users ranged from 3.5 hours per week to 73 hours per week (one librarian held both a full- and part-time reference position). The median for interaction with users was twelve hours per week, with a mean of 19.83 hours. The years of experience in academic reference work ranged from two to ten years, with a median of three years and a mean of 4.72 years. Library experience other than in academic reference ranged from none to twenty-five years, with a median of 5.5 years and a mean of 7.41 years.

Users

Library users were selected as subjects when they interacted with the librarian informants. The twenty-seven interactions selected for analysis included two that had two students working together. Therefore, a total of twenty-nine users were interviewed, thirteen males and sixteen females.[10] They reported ages ranging from sixteen to forty-nine, the mean being 24.65 years. Educational levels of users ranged from five who were attending high school to one Ph. D., who was a faculty member. Thirteen were attending the site institutions. Thirteen others were attending other colleges, and the remaining three were not enrolled in any institution of higher education. The users had a diverse range of academic majors including sciences, social sciences, and liberal arts.

The users came to the library for multiple reasons. All stated that they used the library for research, twenty-one said that they came to borrow materials, and seventeen came to study. Most reported a moderate number of library visits, and the majority (seventeen) required help from the librarian one to three times per semester. Four reported that they had never sought a librarian's help before.

Procedure

At each site, the library administration gave permission to conduct the study and to use a small room or office adjacent to the reference area to set up a tape recorder and conduct the pre- and postinteraction interviews. The researcher conducted interviews over the course of one academic semester with each of the three sites being visited, in rotation, nine times at various hours of the day and evening, including weekends. This was important because the type of user varied from day to evening or from weekday to weekend. For example, at the public college, graduate students and part-time, nontraditional students usually used the library on evenings and weekends.

Time of the semester was another critical element that affected the level of activity at the reference desk and the librarian's amount of available time for each user. Level of activity typically rises and falls during the course of a semester. Also, students have more urgent information needs during the second half of the semester, especially in the last few weeks as deadlines for semester-long projects approach. Preliminary interviews with librarians took place during the first two weeks of the semester. Observations and interviews with librarian–user pairs began in the third week and continued at the rate of two to three interviews per week, with days of the week and hours of the day in rotation, for the remainder of the semester.

In all, the author interviewed the nine librarians four times each, once prior to the reference interaction and three times following the interaction (one with each of three users). The author interviewed the twenty-nine users once, following the selected reference interaction. Table 1 summarizes the interview types and numbers.

The interviews were structured on a list of prepared questions so as to ensure that each participant was asked similar questions and that the interviews centered on the study's research questions.[11] Focus was on the users' perceptions of the interaction—how they thought it went and how useful it was for them. In addition, the author elicited one or two critical incidents (described below) regarding previous interactions and collected demographic data.

During the course of the interviews, the researcher encouraged the participants to be open in their responses.[12] She assured them that:
- Their responses would be kept strictly confidential.
- The study was exploratory and not designed to judge effectiveness.

Table 1
Interview Summary

Librarians

Preinteraction	Postinteraction
3 sites	3 sites
x 3 librarians	x 3 librarians
9 interviews	x 3 site visits
	27 interviews

Subtotal: 9 + 27 = 36

Users

Preinteraction	Postinteraction
	3 sites
none	x 9 visits
	x 1 interview
	27 interviews*

Subtotal: 27

Total: 36 (librarian) + 27 (user) = 63 interviews

*At two interviews, two users were questioned.

Librarians especially were informed that no evaluation of their performance would be made or communicated to their supervisors. Futher, they were assured that the study was being conducted for scholarly research purposes only and that under no circumstances would their names or identifying characteristics be revealed.

Each participant was given a copy of the informed consent and information sheet to sign and keep.[13] In addition, the author assured participants that the interview questions had no "right answer" and that the goal of the interview was to discover their perspectives on reference encounters.

Preinteraction Interview with Librarians

The preinteraction interviews with the nine reference librarians took place prior to the observations of the librarians' interactions with users. The interview questions centered on librarian perceptions of:

- successful and unsuccessful reference interviews;
- critical incidents (described below);
- qualities of good/poor librarians and users;
- the purpose of the reference interview.[14]

Selection of Interactions

After the author finished all the preinteraction interviews, she made three visits to each of the nine librarian participants when each librarian was scheduled to be on reference duty for one hour. In the course of each visit, the author selected an interaction with one user for follow-up interviews with user and librarian. The purpose of these interviews was to record participants' perceptions of the reference interactions.

To give the librarian time to become somewhat used to the presence of the interviewer, she established an observation period lasting twenty minutes.[15] During this time, she observed reference activity and completed Observation Form A.[16]

After twenty minutes of observation, the author selected the next librarian–user interaction of at least two speaking turns for follow-up interviews. The occurrence of at least two speaking turns ensured that the study focused on substantive reference interactions rather than directional queries. The study did not include directional questions such as Where is the pencil sharpener? In the library profession, these are generally not considered to be "reference questions" as defined by Heartsill Young: "Any request by a library user for information or assistance in locating information . . . between the user and a member of the reference staff."[17] As soon as it was determined that each participant had taken two speaking turns, the author filled out Observation Form B.[18]

Study of the interaction began when the user approached the reference desk. The literature review revealed that nonverbal communication, such as the user's perceptions of the librarian as the user approaches the reference desk, is an important part of interpersonal communication.[19] Study of the interaction ended when librarian and user directed their attention away from each other and began to focus on other tasks. As happened on several occasions, if the user had been helped before the selected interaction and had returned to the reference desk for additional help with the same librarian, the researcher considered this encounter as a predecessor of the studied interaction and discussed it in the postinteraction interview.

User Postinteraction Interviews

The author interviewed users immediately following the selected interactions. She invited the user's participation in the study and asked if he or she would be willing to answer a few questions in the nearby room where the tape recorder had been set up.[20] If the user agreed, he or she was taken to the interview room, immediately assured of anonymity, and asked to read and sign an informed consent form. The author then asked the user the prepared questions regarding the interaction that just took place. The answers were recorded on audiotapes that the author immediately numbered and coded for later identification and matching with the appropriate librarian interview.

The postinteraction interview with each user lasted approximately ten to fifteen minutes. The brevity of the interview enabled collection of the desired data with a minimum of intrusion on the user's work. Users were generally very cooperative and generous with their time, with only a few refusing to be interviewed. In cases of refusal, time pressure was given as the reason. For example, some had class in a few minutes or had impending (or past due) deadlines for their assignments. However, on the rare occasion that a user refused, the next user agreed to be interviewed; thus it was never necessary to reschedule a site visit. Only one user was unable to complete all of the interview questions due to interruptions and time pressure.

Librarian Postinteraction Interviews

At the conclusion of each user interview, as soon as the reference librarian was available, the librarian postinteraction interview took place, also away from the reference desk. The purpose of the postinteraction interview was to record the librarian's perceptions of the interaction. The librarians were able to arrange their schedules so that they were on duty at the reference desk for one hour or less with a break afterward to allow the author to conduct the interview as soon after the interaction as possible. In most cases, a second librarian was available, giving the librarian participant flexibility to leave the reference desk for an interview as soon as the user interview was concluded. If another librarian was not available, the researcher waited until the end of the librarian's scheduled hour of duty.

The time lag before the librarian postinteraction interview was fifteen minutes at the least (the time it took to interview the user) and forty minutes at most (possible wait until the end of the librarian's hour of desk duty). Interviews of reference librarians could not take place directly following the interaction because the user had to be interviewed first and sometimes the librarians had to finish their hour stints at the desk. The optimum procedure would have been an interview with the librarian immediately following the interaction, but the logistics of the study precluded this choice. Because the interview with the librarians was delayed, their memory of the details of the particular interaction sometimes lost some clarity. This is a limitation of the study design and available resources. If for any reason the librarian hesitated in remembering the interaction, he or she was prompted. This prompting consisted of a brief description of the topic of the reference question. The librarians remembered the interactions with minimal prompting, usually with no prompting at all, because they could see the author's approach to the user and because generally the time lapse was only fifteen to twenty minutes.

When the interviewer was certain that the librarian recalled the selected interaction, she asked the librarian the postinteraction questions.[21] As in the librarian's preinteraction interview, the interviewer asked questions that were structured and open-ended in nature. She also asked probes or follow-up questions, as appropriate. These would generally take the form of asking the librarian to clarify or provide more description for statements that were vague. If the interviewer observed something unusual in the interaction, additional questions would explore this.[22] The researcher also recorded these interviews on audiotape for later transcription and coded them for later identification.

Data Collection Forms

In addition to the interview questions, the data collection instruments consisted of Observation Forms A and B, and demographic data collection forms for librarians and users.

Observation Form A: Contextual Data

In addition to collecting interview data, the researcher observed the activity at the reference desk for twenty minutes before selecting an interaction. This observation provided a context for the librarian–user interactions. The researcher noted information about the activity at the reference desk, including the number of users interacting with the librarian, the number of phone queries, and any additional activities taking place (e.g., computer maintenance, interaction with staff or student assistants). The researcher also completed one Observation Form A for each twenty-minute period of observation.[23]

Observation Form B: Specific Interaction

The researcher also collected data on each interaction's length, the topic of the reference query, and any additional details using Observation Form B.[24] These data provided cues, if necessary, to prompt a librarian who could not immediately recall a selected interaction.

Analysis

The interview transcripts[25] provided the primary form of data used in analysis.[26] The author's handwritten field notes, Observation Forms A and B, and demographic forms recorded supplemental data. The analysis focused on the four research questions centering on the exploration of the importance of the relational versus content dimensions of communication in the library–user encounter. The author used three methods for analysis:

- development of a category scheme, reflecting the relational and content dimensions of the librarian–user encounter;
- examination of critical incidents;
- comparison of the user and librarian paired perceptions of the interactions.

This multiple-method approach provided a validity check and added to the credibility of the results.[27] Procedures and results for each of these methods are described in chapters 5 through 7.

Notes

1. See Marie L. Radford, "Relational Aspects of Reference Interactions: A Qualitative Investigation of the Perceptions of Users and Librarians in the Academic Library" (Ph. D. diss., Rutgers—State Univ. of New Jersey, 1993), for a fuller description of the pilot study methodology and results.

2. These librarians (one male and one female) had a mean age of forty-five years and were both full-time reference librarians with an average of 6.25 years of experience in academic reference. Both held two master's degrees, one in library science and philosophy and one in library science and psychology.

3. The author recruited three user informants by asking for volunteers from classes engaging in research projects requiring library work and librarian contact. The one male and two female volunteers had a mean age of thirty-nine years. One was an undergraduate senior, two were graduate students. Two majored in elementary education, one in business. All three used the library a moderate amount (from one to five times per month)to do research and to study.

4. John C. Flanagan, "The Critical Incident Technique," *Psychological Bulletin* 51 (July 1954): 327–58.

5. See Radford, "Relational Aspects of Reference Interactions," for the preliminary outline of categories.

6. See Radford, "Relational Aspects of Reference Interactions," for the pilot study critical incident results.

7. For a thorough treatment of qualitative research methods and questions of reliability and validity, see Jerome Kirk and Marc L. Miller, *Reliability and Validity in Qualitative Research* (Beverly Hills, Calif.: Sage, 1986); Norman K. Denzin, *Sociological Methods: A Sourcebook* (Chicago: Aldine, 1970).

8. See Denzin, *Sociological Methods*.

9. See appendix A.

10. See appendix A.

11. See appendix C.

12. See Grant McCracken, *The Long Interview* (Newbury Park, Calif.: Sage, 1988); Constance A. Mellon, *Naturalistic Inquiry for Library Science: Methods and Applications for Research, Evaluation, and Teaching* (New York: Greenwood, 1990).

13. See appendix B.

14. See appendix C.

15. Morton Deutsch, "An Experimental Study of the Effects of Co-operation and Completion upon Group Process," *Human Relations* 2 (July 1949): 199–231; Eugene J. Webb, Donald T. Campbell, Richard D. Schwartz, and Lee Sechrest, *Unobtrusive Measures: Nonreactive Research in the Social Sciences* (Chicago: Rand McNally, 1966), have noted that this period of acclimation can reduce the contaminating effect of the observer on the data.

16. See appendix D.

17. Heartsill Young, *The ALA Glossary of Library and Information Science* (Chicago: ALA, 1983), 188.

18. See appendix D.

19. See Judee K. Burgoon, David B. Buller, and W. Gill Woodall, *Nonverbal Communication: The Unspoken Dialogue* (New York: Harper & Row, 1989); Marie L. Radford, "A Qualitative Investigation of Nonverbal Immediacy in the User's Decision to Approach the Academic Reference Librarian," presented at the Library Research Seminar I, Florida State Univ., Tallahassee, Fla., Nov. 1–2, 1996.

20. The original plan was to have conducted the postinteraction interview with the user in the reference area and then ask the user if he or she had time for additional, extended post-interaction questions that would be tape-recorded. This turned out to be logistically difficult. The author interviewed the first user in this way and was interrupted, which resulted in an unfinished interview. In addition, the reference area was quite noisy. The next user agreed to be tape-recorded from the beginning, and the author decided to proceed with all users in this fashion.

21. See appendix C.

22. In one case, for example, as the librarian was helping one user with a reference source, a second user was trying to get the librarian's attention for about one minute. When the librarian did not respond, the second user walked away. The researcher asked the librarian if she did not see the second user or if she saw the

second user but chose to ignore him. The librarian answered that she did not notice that someone was waiting. An interesting discussion followed on the librarian's perceptions of the appropriate way to approach a reference librarian for help.

23. See appendix D.

24. See appendix D.

25. The author transcribed the audiotape recordings of all interviews verbatim or, in some cases, partially. Partial transcriptions omitted portions deemed to be unrelated to research questions (such as discussions of the weather) or that gave excessive detail (such as the minutiae of searching strategy). The author briefly summarized and noted the omitted portions in the transcripts.

26. See appendix E. Sample rather than complete transcripts are being appended to protect the anonymity of the sources. Entire transcripts may reveal identities, especially to supervisors of librarian participants, and some transcripts contain intimate material.

27. See John Brewer and Albert Hunter, *Multimethod Research: A Synthesis of Styles* (Newbury Park, Calif.: Sage, 1989).

Chapter 5

Development and Results of the Category Scheme

◦◦ ◦◦ ◦◦ ◦◦ ◦◦ ◦◦ ◦◦ ◦◦ ◦◦

*T*he author used the preliminary outline of categories developed in the pilot study (see chapter 4) as a basis for the first analysis of the interview data collected in the main study. The final outline of categories (see appendix G) is a highly detailed, organized list of topics found in the user and librarian interviews. It was constructed through the author's careful reading of the transcripts, identifying and categorizing the topics discussed by librarians and users.[1] The goal was to develop a description of the librarian–user interaction that would be useful in addressing the research questions. According to Grant McCracken:

> The object of analysis is to determine the categories, relationships, and assumptions that informs [sic] the respondent's view of the world in general and the topic in particular.[2]

For analysis of interview data, the study adapted a framework suggested by McCracken. As the investigator listened to the tapes and read the transcripts, she noted topics, discussed by the interviewees, that suggested potential categories. The author identified words and phrases that related to relational/interpersonal factors as well as those indicating content/technical factors. For example, when a user spoke about a librarian who was "friendly," this was categorized as relational; when a librarian spoke of users who "knew exactly what they were looking for," this was classified as relating to content.

At the second stage, the author reviewed the words and phrases tentatively classified as relational or content. She then compared them to one another, looking for relationships or patterns of similarities. When two or more users or librarians made similar comments, these were grouped together. As these groups of similar comments were identified, the author organized them into the outline of categories. For example, every time a user mentioned a librarian having a positive attitude (such as being helpful, patient, caring, cooperative), these comments would be grouped together under the category "positive attitude toward user." In this way, the large amount of transcript data was reduced to a well-organized and coherent outline summarizing the interviews. In the last stage, the researcher further examined the categories to find their interrelationships. As McCracken explains:

> Some of these themes will be redundant, and the best formulation should be chosen while the others are eliminated. The remainder can then be organized hierarchically. One or two themes will be the chief points under which the remainder of the themes can be subsumed.[3]

Through analysis and data reduction the author was able to identify generalized relations between categories (hypotheses) which will enable future observation to focus more precisely.[4]

As noted in chapter 3, in analyzing the interview data from the pilot study, the investigator identified three themes (major categories): goals, facilitators, and barriers. These themes provided a starting point for analysis and description of findings. As the author identified topics described by the interviewees related to each theme, she added them to the outline of categories.[5]

In naming the categories, the participants' own words were used whenever possible. When participants' words did not provide a succinct label, the researcher used her own words. Usually this was necessary to name broader categories that grouped similar ideas. For example, if a user said that a librarian was "responsive" or "a good listener," this word and this phrase were placed into an author-created category: "good communication skills." The transcripts were color-coded using an adaptation of the MAT (multichromatic analysis technique).[6] This technique involves use of colored markers and colored paper clips as aids to analysis. The MAT allowed the researcher to organize efficiently and access a large amount of qualitative data. In addition, whenever a transcript repeated a theme or category that had previously emerged, that repetition was noted in the outline. If a transcript described a new category, it would be added to the outline. Categories were marked with the number of librarians (L) and/or users (U) who mentioned each factor. Subcategories were listed in the order of most frequently mentioned first so that the most critical factors could be easily identified.

In this manner, the author analyzed and coded the nine pre- and twenty-seven postinteraction interviews with the librarians. In addition, portions of the pre- and postinteraction interviews were analyzed using the critical incident technique and the analysis of paired perceptions, described below.

Category Scheme Results

As in the pilot study, three major themes emerged in the final outline of categories:

- goals or aims of the interaction;
- facilitators: qualities that enhance goals, communication;
- barriers: characteristics that impede goals, communication.

Both library users and librarians perceived the reference encounter to be a highly complex process. This can be seen in the intricate and fine-grained nature of the subcategories under each of the main categories. As can be seen in appendix G, the outline of categories was very lengthy. Key portions of the outline relating to each of the major themes are summarized and discussed below.

Theme 1. Goals or Aims of the Interaction[7]
Librarian Goals

Evidence provided by the informants in the pilot study led the author to conceptualize librarian–user interaction as instances of goal-directed communication. *Goals* were defined as the participants' stated aims or outcomes for the interaction. The interviewer asked both users and librarians to discuss their goals for the reference interaction. All eleven librarians interviewed (nine librarians from the main study plus two from the pilot study) expressed more than one goal, which were grouped into seven different categories:

- problem definition;
- developing strategies for solving the problem;

Table 2
Representative Librarian Responses Related to
Goals or Aims of the Interaction Theme[8]

Problem Definition
"To find out what the patron needs to know." (L01)

"To determine what the exact information is that they're looking for and to get a complete understanding of what their actual question is." (L03)

Developing Strategies for Solving the Problem
"To assist the patron in securing that information." (L02)

"To steer them in that direction and explain how it is that they would find it." (L05)

Enablement
"To get them to be an independent searcher to have an idea of how they can do this for themselves next time or at least a little more independently." (L07)

"To try to teach them as you go along with the question so that they become more independent library users." (L03)

"To try to explain a little bit about how libraries are organized and how information is organized in the library and how that...they can find what they want in the library." (L05)

Developing Positive Attitude toward Library Program
"I was also hoping that he would be pleased that we were trying something new rather than sticking to the other [bibliographic instruction program]." (L01)

Gaining User's Confidence
"Gaining the confidence that yes, indeed, he could broaden his research after having identified some of the information." (L02)

Table 2 cont.

Composite of Above Goals

"Try and interpret what it is, the kind of information they need to know, and lead them in a direction where they can find what it is that they need." (Pilot Librarian A)

Goal Dependent upon Context

"Well, I think it depends on where you're working and who they [the users] are." (L03)

- enablement (helping users to be independent);
- developing the user's positive attitude toward library program;
- gaining user's confidence;
- composite of above goals;
- goal dependent upon context of question.

Table 2 provides examples of librarians' goal statements.

User Goals

In contrast to the librarians, users had two basic goal categories:

- developing strategies for solving the problem;
- enablement.

In addition, one user believed, along with two of the librarians, that the goal was dependent on context. Table 3 gives examples of users' goal statements.

There was greater diversity of goals for the librarians than the users, although there was much similarity in the goals that were expressed by both. Table 4 summarizes and compares the goals of librarians and users.

As can be seen in table 4, the large majority of the goals for both users and librarians were centered on content dimensions. For librarians, problem definition, developing strategies for solving the problem, and enablement were the three highest-ranked categories, with a majority of the librarians aiming for each. Two librarian goals, developing positive attitude toward library program and gaining user's confidence, were relational in nature. These two relational goals were mentioned by one librarian each, so nine out of eleven librarians focused exclusively on the content dimension in their goals.

All of the users expressed their goals in terms of content dimensions. The vast majority of users, twenty-six (86%), mentioned developing strate-

---

Table 3
Representative User Responses Related to
Goals or Aims of the Interaction Theme

Developing Strategies for Solving the Problem
"Just direction. There's a lot of times that I'm researching things and no idea where to find them in the library." (U07)

"To help me find my information if not to know where I can find it; if it's not here, find it at another library." (U09)

"Try to pinpoint something, look for sources that I wasn't quite sure about." (U10)

"To get a push kinda to save time." (U27)

"To find information that maybe I've been looking for on my own." (Pilot User A)

"To do the best job I can as far as like locating the material that will help me do my job." (Pilot User B)

Enablement
"To going about different sources so maybe next time I could even do it myself a little bit." (U16)

---

gies for solving the problem as their goal. The librarians' highest-ranked category, problem definition, was not found among the users' goal statements.

Theme 2. Facilitators: Qualities That Enhance Goals, Communication[9]

The second major theme was facilitators: qualities that enhance goals, communication. *Facilitators* are defined as qualities or characteristics that have a positive impact on the perceptions of the participants in the interaction.

Although some facilitators affect content, most are relational factors. Interviewees described relational facilitators with greater frequency and in more detail than they did content facilitators. Thus, the interpersonal dimension was a greater concern for both users and librarians despite their both having goals that focused primarily on content issues.

Table 4
Goals of Librarians and Users

Goal	Librarians (N=11)****		Users(N=32)****	
Problem definition	9 (82%)*	(C)	0	
Developing strategies	7 (64%)	(C)	26 (86%)	(C)
Enablement	6 (55%)	(C)	3 (10%)	(C)
Attitude	1 (9%)	(R)	0	
Confidence	1 (9%)	(R)	0	
Composite	3 (27%)**		0	
Context	2 (18%)**		1 (3%)	(C)
Total	29***		30*****	

C=Content R=Relational

* All percentages are rounded to the nearest whole.
** Unable to determine if content or relational because librarians did not specify.
*** Total exceeds N because librarians gave multiple goals.
**** Includes main study and pilot study participants.
***** Total is less than N because two users did not specify goals.

Librarians' Content-Related Facilitators

Librarians said that their knowledge base and that of users facilitates the transfer of content in reference interactions. Librarians described the user's knowledge base in terms of:
- general knowledge;
- specialized knowledge, such as understanding of the research process, libraries, and their information need.

Librarians also discussed their own knowledge base in terms of:
- general knowledge;
- specialized knowledge, such as awareness of specialized reference sources and the library's collection.

Table 5 provides representative librarians' comments on the importance of the users' and librarians' knowledge base as facilitators.

Users' Content-Related Facilitators

There were similarities between the librarian and user content-related facilitators, but there were also dimensions that only users noted. Both dis-

---

Table 5
Representative Librarian Responses Related to
Facilitators–Content Factors

User's Knowledge Base
"I always enjoy working with someone who has broad knowledge." (L04)

"They have some overall sense [of] how the library works." (L09)

"Knowing exactly, or a[s] close as possible, know exactly what they are looking for." (L02)

Librarian's Knowledge Base
"I think standard knowledge of the sources and all the basic subject areas." (L03)

"You have to know your library." (L01)

"They have to know the structure of information one assumes that they do and know certain sources our library uses consistently." (L05)

---

cussed knowledge base as an important category, but users' perceptions of the librarians' knowledge base were much less detailed than those of the librarians. Users did not discuss general knowledge, but half of them mentioned the importance of the librarians' specialized knowledge, especially knowledge of information sources. Another subcategory, information, emerged from the user's point of view, dealing with the librarians' ability to:

- provide information delivery;
- provide information access;
- fill an information need;
- be product oriented.

Table 6 provides a sample of users' comments regarding the information and knowledge base facilitators.

Table 7 provides a summary and comparison of the content-related facilitators for librarians and users. As shown, librarians' two highest-ranked categories were related to the knowledge base of users and librarians. More users, however, were focused on the information category, which dealt with

---

Table 6
Representative User Responses Related to
Facilitators–Content Factors

Information Related

"You know they've always ended up finding something for me, or telling me where I could get it, or calling another library." (U24)

"He went right to the books and showed me exactly where they were." (U23)

"Giving me the book, opening it up, and telling me this is what you want, this is what you need, and to tell me exactly what kind of subject to look under and not something vague, something really specific." (U04)

Knowledge Base

"She knew right where to go . . . which computer to access the information." (U08)

"She's very resourceful." (U18)

"Even if it wasn't necessarily his field, he knew how to help." (U22)

Table 7
Content-Related Facilitators for Librarians and Users

Category	Librarians (N=11)*	Users (N=32)*
Knowledge Base		
of users	7L (64%)	0
of librarians	11L (100%)	11U (34%)
Information		
of librarians	1L (9%)	18U (56%)
Total	19L**	29U***

  * Includes main study and pilot study participants.
 ** Total exceeds N because librarians gave multiple facilitators.
*** Total is less than N because three users did not specify content-related facilitators.

information delivery and access. However, the librarians knowledge base was also an important factor.

Librarians' Relational Facilitators

In the category of facilitators–relational, both librarians and users have a more detailed, richer scheme than that developed in the facilitators–content area.

For librarians and users, there were three major subcategories under the facilitators–relational category:
- attitude;
- relationship quality;
- approachability.

The attitude category was defined as the perceptions of the demeanor of the other participant in the interaction. It is important to note that perceptions of attitude were inferred by the informants from the verbal and nonverbal communication of the person with whom they interacted. In other words, participants inferred internal attitudes from external cues. Under attitude, further subcategories were:
- positive attitude toward user, such as librarians being helpful, patient, and reassuring;
- positive attitude toward task, such as users being serious, motivated, and persistent, and librarians being excited, interested, and professional.

The relationship quality category was defined as perceptions of the interpersonal dynamics of the interaction. The *approachability* category dealt with perceptions of positive nonverbal behavior such as eye contact and smiling. Table 8 provides examples of librarians discussing relational factors as facilitators.

Users' Relational Facilitators

Users also had a more detailed, richer range of categories for facilitators–relational than for facilitators–content. Attitude emerged as an important category for users. Table 9 provides examples of user responses centering on these relational factors.

Table 10 compares the responses of librarians and users on relational facilitators and emphasizes the importance of attitude in the interaction. Ten librarians (91%) and twenty-four users (75%) discussed attitude as im-

---

Table 8
Representative Librarian Responses Related to
Facilitators–Relational Factors

User's Attitude

" Afterwards, she came up to me and said 'this was great.' She really, she showed enthusiasm. Her face looked as if it was Christmas, and you know that's the kind of reward that we get." (Pilot Librarian B)

"I find that if they're motivated, then I'm motivated." (L09)

"Being persistent and I guess being patient, too, because it may be new to them and they may not understand initially what's going on." (L05)

"Having a certain confidence in the fact that the user is at the library and attempting to accomplish something... the determination to accomplish, to set ones' goals." (L02)

Relationship Quality

"She was willing to explain those things [when] I asked her questions." (L08)

"The willingness to trust the librarian whether it be a confidential matter or just something that they weren't really comfortable talking about." (L03)

"I like it when they accept my authority." (L06)

"I guess I do like users that aren't afraid to dig in ... people that are clearly interested and excited by the fact that they've managed to find something or by the quest, tends to turn me on a little more, too, and I get more excited about it." (L07)

---

portant. Relationship quality also drew comments from ten librarians (91%) and sixteen users (50%). Both users and librarians mentioned many of the relational qualities. Librarians placed greater emphasis on the *user's* attitude and relationship qualities. This finding is contrasted

Table 9
Representative User Responses Related to
Facilitators–Relational Factors

Librarian's Attitude

"She was really helpful and she came over . . . she made an extra effort to come over and she was funny, I mean she had a really nice personality." (U17)

"He was just very helpful. You know, it wasn't like I wasn't like a bother to him . . . that's their job, and sometimes you go to them and it's a bother, you know, hey, that's what you're here for." (U13)

"She was a very nice lady; she treated me like she wanted to be treated herself, you know, with respect." (U19)

"To be pleasant, to be attentive to my needs, to be *with* me while I'm asking for what I want. Polite, kindness, courtesies, I'm another human being on the other side of this interaction and I expect to be respected as such, but know that the person on the other side has information that I need so we have to connect together." (Pilot User B)

Relationship Quality

"She stayed a few extra minutes to help me get the forms so I could go and get the books and I was in a time crunch . . . and she didn't give me a hard time about it, she was interested more in helping me than in getting home." (U21)

"Getting involved showing that, not that you're wholly enthused, you know, but at least that you care, you're not just there." (U27)

"She did more than I asked her to, she took me where I had to go and didn't just show me, and she made sure I understood what I was doing." (U04)

"Having a librarian who was willing to take the time, sit down, and go over with me until I was really sure about what I was doing." (Pilot User A)

Approachability

"I was impressed that she got up and went around the desk and took me back to the reference section instead of just telling me." (U21)

Table 10 Relational Facilitators for Librarians and Users		
Category	Librarians (N=11)*	Users (N=32)*
Attitude		
of user	10L (91%)	0
of librarian	9L (82%)	24U (75%)
Relationship quality		
of user	10L (91%)	0
of librarian	9L (82%)	16U (50%)
Approachability		
of user	0	0
of librarian	3L (27%)	2U (7%)
Total	41L**	42U**

 * Includes main study and pilot study participants.
** Total exceeds N because users and librarians discussed multiple relational factors.

with users who tended to emphasize perceptions of the *librarian's* attitude, relationship quality, and approachability.

Information Retrieval Technologies as Facilitators
An additional category was the effects of information technologies on the reference interaction. In the pilot interviews, both librarians mentioned this factor. Because the literature review also indicated that computerized information retrieval technologies would be increasingly used in reference interactions, the librarians in the main study were asked to comment on their impact. Librarians perceived information retrieval systems as both facilitators and barriers to the reference process. Because the researcher asked the librarians directly about technology, they discussed it more than the users, who were not asked directly.

The information technologies as facilitators category had content components, mostly focused on the ease of retrieval and the depth of information retrieved. There were also relational aspects, centered on the impact technology has on interpersonal interaction. The librarians disagreed on the nature of this impact. Perceptions varied from one librarian who felt

---

Table 11

Representative Responses Related to Librarian and User Perceptions of Information Technologies as Facilitators to Goal Achievement

---

Content Factors–Librarians

"Oh, definitely, they've [information technologies] had an impact. I think it opens up a lot . . . sometimes it makes it a lot easier to find what you're looking for." (L03)

"They've certainly enhanced my ability to provide information more efficiently, and just the breadth and the depth of the information has increased." (L04)

"CD-ROMs help enormously in that they really do, they just made the process a lot easier . . . they have more complete information." (L05)

Content Factors–Users

"Obviously, the computer as a tool is just a big time-saver." (U08)

"The computer . . . it just had lots of great sources . . . for us to look at, you know, just many, many of them." (U03)

Relational Factors–Librarians

"It's a lot more labor-intensive." (L05)

"It has changed the entire interaction . . . the interaction is more intensive . . . perhaps doubled." (L02)

"Because of . . . this access to more information, the patron who is genuinely interested gets really excited and starts digging in much more than he or she might have if it was paper sources." (L04)

Relational Factors–Users

"The computer is fun." (U3)

---

that they had no effect on the basic interaction to another who felt they have totally changed the interaction. Table 11 gives examples of statements dealing with information technologies as facilitators in the inter-

Table 12 Information Technology as Facilitator				
Category	Librarians (N=11)*		Users (N=32)*	
Content factors			**Content factors**	
Impact on search process	9L	(82%)	Librarian knowledgeable about systems	2U (6%)
Impact on information retrieval	3L	(27%)	Librarian demonstrates how to work computer	2U (6%)
			Computer big time-saver	1U (3%)
Relational factors			**Relational factors**	
Impact on relationship	9L	(82%)	Computer is fun	1U (3%)
Total	21L**			6U***

   * Includes main and pilot study participants.

  ** Total exceeds N because librarians gave multiple facilitators. Librarians were asked directly about impact of technology, but users were not.

*** Total is less than N because not all users specified information technology as facilitator.

action. Table 12 provides a summary for comparison of the categories of librarians and users.

Theme 3. Barriers: Characteristics That Impede Goals, Communication[10]

The third major theme—barriers: characteristics that impede goals, communication—brings together factors that participants reported to have fostered negative perceptions of reference encounters. *Barriers* are qualitites or characteristics that had a negative impact on the perceptions of the participants.

Librarians' Content-Related Barriers

The librarians' barriers related to content dimensions were much more diversified than the users'. Librarians focused more than users on the lack of a knowledge base as the cause of unsuccessful reference interactions. Librarians identified the following as content-related barriers regarding users' knowledge base:

Table 13
Representative Librarian and User Responses Related to Barriers–Content Factors

Librarians about Users

"The other problem you have here a lot is with international students for whom the whole process of communication is sometimes a frustrating one . . . the language barrier there is very difficult sometimes." (L08)

"They don't understand indexes at all." (L09)

"They don't know what they want, so no matter how much of a reference interview I did, I could never find it out." (L03)

"The poor library . . . user is one that has not done the proper preparatory work, has not . . . read the assignment prior to the reference interview and then proceeding to thrust the assignment in front of the librarian's eyes and expecting immediate digestion and comprehension of what the ultimate aim is." (L02)

Users about Librarians

"I guess she didn't have any knowledge in the area . . . if the librarian doesn't know about it, then she can't really help you with it." (U04)

"She wasn't apparently as comfortable with the computer, and she didn't know exactly how to do it for me." (U08)

Table 14
Content-Related Barriers for Librarians and Users

Category	Librarians (N=11)*	Users (N=32)*
Knowledge base		
of users	7L (64%)	1U (3%)
of librarians	5L (45%)	2U (7%)
Information		
of librarians	0	1U (3%)
Total	12L**	4U***

  * Includes main and pilot study participants.
 ** Total exceeds N because librarians gave multiple barriers.
*** Total is less than N because not all users specified content-related barriers.

- User lacks general knowledge (e.g., of English language in the case of international students).
- User lacks specialized knowledge of basic library structure, the research process, and the assignments.
- User lacks ability to articulate need.

In addition, librarians identified the following as content-related barriers regarding librarians' knowledge base:

- Librarian lacks specialized knowledge, including subject knowledge and knowledge of the collection.
- Librarian lacks experience.
- Librarian is unprepared.
- Librarian is not up to date.
- Librarian lacks knowledge of information retrieval tools, electronic sources, and specialized sources (e.g., business and legal tools).

Table 13 provides a sample of statements related to this category.

Users' Content-Related Barriers

Users reported very few perceptions of barriers formed by content factors. Their negative perceptions were centered more on relational factors, which are discussed below. As in the facilitators theme, the librarians and users both had perceptions dealing with knowledge base. In addition, one user reported a barrier related to lack of information delivery. Table 13 provides a sample of statements related to this category.

Table 14 provides a summary for comparison of content-related barriers identified by librarians and users.

Librarians' Relational Barriers

Relational qualities were critical to perceptions of barriers to success. Relational aspects as barriers were discussed with even greater frequency and detail than facilitators. Librarians spoke of more numerous and diverse categories of negative user attitude toward librarian than of negative user attitude toward task. This result is the opposite of the findings for facilitators and suggests that for librarians, positive attitude toward task was an important measure for success, but negative user attitude toward librarian was more likely to be a factor in failure. Table 15 provides examples of librarians' comments related to relational barriers.

Table 15
Representative Librarian Responses Related to
Barriers–Relational Factors

Negative Attitude

"If a student shows impatience, inattentiveness . . . his or her seriousness in actually finding an answer and giving time, I think that's a personality that unfortunately is lacking in many students today." (L02)

"People who approach you and they're angry and hostile, you know, that doesn't help because when you're trying to communicate with someone . . . I think that's when you're off to a really bad start." (L03)

"I think the people that are harder to work with don't want to be bothered finding what it is they need . . . don't want to go through the steps . . . some of the students are reluctant users of the library. They have an assignment to do and they really don't care about it." (L05)

"A person who is here under duress well, they've got this assignment. They *have* to go to the library because it's the only place where this information that they need is available and they *have* to write this paper and they resent every minute of it." (Pilot Librarian B)

Poor Relationship Quality

"They really expect to be handed everything, and that's become far more prevalent in the last couple of years." (L07)

"[Poor users are] the ones who wait until two days before the assignment is due before they start thinking about it." (L06)

"People have a tendency not to understand that the librarian needs certain information to make it a more prosperous, successful session at the reference desk." (L02)

Users' Relational Barriers

Like librarians, the users' categories for relational barriers were fuller than the content barriers. The same categories were present, but there were differences in degree of importance. For example, compare the users' emphasis on librarians' lack of approachability mentioned by fifteen users (47%), but only three librarians (27%) (see table 16). In addition, under negative attitude, users' subcategories included: evades user, resists user, and resists interaction. These were not present in the librarians' interviews.

Table 17 provides examples of user statements classified as relational factors under the barriers theme. For users and librarians, the same categories for facilitators were also present in the barriers theme, although cast negatively:

• negative attitude, including negative attitude toward librarian (by user) or toward user (by librarian) and negative attitude toward task;

• Poor relationship quality, including user rejecting librarian, user lacking in self-disclosure, poor communication skills, not process oriented;

• lack of approachability, including negative nonverbal behavior and avoiding user contact.

Responses of librarians and users regarding relational barriers are compared in table 16. Higher percentages of the librarians commented on rela-

Table 16 Relational Barriers for Librarians and Users		
Category	Librarians (N=11)*	Users (N=32)*
Negative attitude of user		
toward librarian	8L (73%)	3U (9%)
toward task	5L (45%)	2U (6%)
Negative attitude of librarian		
toward user	8L (73%)	9U (28%)
toward task	7L (64%)	6U (19%)
Poor relationship quality		
of user	10L (91%)	0
of librarian	7L (64%)	9U (28%)
Lack of approachability		
of user	0	0
of librarian	3L (27%)	15U (47%)
Total	45L**	44U**

* Includes main study and pilot study participants.
** Total exceeds N because users and librarians discussed multiple relational factors.

Table 17
Representative User Responses Related to Barriers–Relational Factors

<u>Negative Attitude</u>
"If the librarian came on strong, with an attitude of mumbled something about [annoyed voice, under the breath grumble] 'can't find it in the card catalog' or anything that would belittle me as an individual in body language or in verbal response would put up my guard and make me feel less of a person at that time and would make my back go up and I wouldn't want to continue with the event that was taking place." (Pilot User C)

"Well, some librarians are really sour and they're like 'Well why don't you do your own research?'" (U10)

"They just didn't want to get involved." (U09)

"They're not very patient toward 'freshpeople.'" (U15)

<u>Poor Relationship Quality</u>
"She was just, you know, 'Oh, did you look in such and such a place first?' and I say 'Oh no.' 'Well, why don't you look there and then get back to me, did you even *bother* to check the card catalog?' Or they say things like . . . well, I'll go 'Oh no, well, you know I came to you for help.'" (U13)

"Some librarians, like, they don't have a lot to say; it's quick, it's like a yes or no answer." (U27)

"The librarian was so busy, caught up in what she was doing, she . . . didn't have time to help just to show you or direct you where you should go . . . she should have at least took the time out, she could get back to whatever she was doing at a later time." (U03)

<u>Lack of Approachability</u>
"They're just like 'Wait a minute' and they're just sitting there talking to somebody, you know, really rude." (U15)

"They stare, and it makes you kind of uncomfortable." (U17)

Table 17 cont.
"They're sipping … something to eat, something to drink … and they're like 'Oh, alright' and … they give you this like, their body language, their facial expressions, they don't have to come right out and say, it's just like the way they present themselves." (U13)

Table 18
Information Retrieval Technology as Barrier

Category	Librarians (N=11)*		Users (N=32)*	
Content factors			**Content factors**	
Negative impact on search process	4L	(36%)	Librarian uncomfortable with computers	1U (3%)
Negative impact on information retrieval	2L	(18%)	Librarian lacks knowledge of computer systems	1U (3%)
Negative impact of maintenance routines	4L	(36%)	Librarian resists technological change	1U (3%)
			Hardware may malfunction	1U (3%)
Relational factors			**Relational factors**	
Fosters user dependence on librarian	1L	(9%)	User uncomfortable with computers	1U (3%)
Made reference interview more difficult	2L	(18%)		
Total	13L**			5U***

* Includes main and pilot study participants.
** Total exceeds N because librarians gave multiple barriers. Librarians were directly asked about impact of technology, but users were not.
*** Total is less than N because not all users specified information technology as barrier.

tional barriers than users. Negative attitude toward librarian (eight librarians, 73%) and poor relationship quality (ten librarians, 91%) were among the highest percentages. For users, the highest percentage related to the librarians' lack of approachability (fifteen users, 47%).

Table 19
Representative Librarian Perceptions of Information
Retrieval Technologies as Barriers

"[information technology] has changed the entire interaction . . . from a skill perspective the interaction is more intensive . . . the products were developed ultimately with hope that they would perhaps speed up and or shorten the . . . interaction, but it seems to have had, at least in this point in time, the opposite [effect]." (L02)

"Even with the kids who are computer smart, they don't know, they haven't the understanding of how you search." (L01)

"In some ways, they've made my job so much easier and in some ways, they've made my job so much harder . . . harder by their very nature and by . . . administrative responses . . . to deal with hardware and software problems." (L06)

"People's expectations have been raised . . . you give them a database and all of a sudden they expect it to be a complete database . . . and there is this sort of continuing naive user that believes that if it's in the computer, it must be so. It's the sort of naivete that used to be attached to books." (L06)

"There's a lot of technical things that can go wrong that might not go wrong in printed index." (L05)

"I went over to OCLC . . . and it was slow and she [a user] was very impatient . . . I hope that she realized that I'm only human, and I was trying to make a machine work." (Pilot Librarian B)

Information Retrieval Technologies as Barriers

The category of effects of information technologies on reference interactions was evident in both the barriers and facilitators categories. Again, because they were asked directly about the impact of information technologies, librarians provided most of the responses (see table 18). According to the librarians these technologies, at times, have had a negative impact on the search process, information retrieval, and on work flow. Librarians attributed

---

Table 20
Representative User Perceptions of
Information Technologies as Barriers

"She wasn't apparently as comfortable with the computer, and she didn't know how to do it for me." (U08)

"I'm just not very comfortable with the computers." (U16)

"Sometimes they [the librarians] have trouble with the computers . . . sometimes just even the mechanical part of it with the changing the paper or something." (U07)

---

this mainly to the need to provide technical support in the event of software or hardware problems. Some also felt that the presence of the technologies resulted in the reference interaction taking more time because it was necessary to teach both the mechanics of searching and the approach by subject. Tables 19 and 20 give examples of responses related to this theme.

External Constraints as Barriers

Both librarians and users mentioned may factors that were either preexisting conditions or external constraints that had a negative impact. These responses were grouped under the category external constraints that form barriers to goal achievement[11] and had the following four subcategories:
- lack of time;
- lack of resources;
- distracting level of activity in library;
- uncomfortable physical facility, environment.
Table 21 provides examples of these categories.

As can be seen in the presentation of the detailed outline of categories, every effort was made to preserve the high level of complexity of the responses and of as many key concepts as possible. Additional discussion of these findings is provided in chapter 8.

Notes

1. The author placed the interview transcripts into notebooks sequentially, preinteraction interviews with librarians 01 to 09 and postinteraction interviews with librarians and users 01 to 27. She also placed librarian and user transcripts for

---

Table 21
Representative Librarian and User Responses–External
Constraints That Form Barriers

Lack of Time
"We have people who come in and then say 'Oh, I really have to run and I don't have time to do it now.'" (L08)

Lack of Resources
"Our collection is not geared to support that question . . . A lot of it [the failure] had to do with the collection, the strength of the collection." (L06)

Distracting Level of Activity in Library
"It was very busy, the microfilm machines were breaking, the phone was ringing, there were a lot of people ." (L09)

Uncomfortable Physical Facility, Environment
"It's just the fact that all these books are here. I don't know, sometimes I feel, especially here, it's very stuffy, the library's very hot. I mean it's been twenty degrees out there, and I've been in here and I've been hot." (U18)

---

each interaction together along with completed Observation Forms A and B, and user and librarian demographic data forms. In this way, all data for each interaction were placed together for analysis. This organization was further facilitated through use of tabs of colored paper and attached to the top of each of the different forms. Each form had a different color assigned to it. For each interview, the number of the interaction plus the "L" for librarian or "U" for user was marked on these colored slips of paper attached to the first page. This make it possible to quickly locate the transcript and supplementary data for each member of an interaction.

2. Grant McCracken, *The Long Interview* (Newbury Park, Calif.: Sage, 1988), 42.

3. Ibid., 46.

4. These hypotheses and future directions will be discussed more fully in chapter 9. See Hope J. Leichter and Vera Hamid-Buglione, *An Examination of Cognitive Processes in Everyday Family Life* (New York: Columbia University, Elbenwood Center for the Study of the Family as Educator, 1983) ERIC Document 226 849.

5. For a more in-depth discussion of the procedure for developing the outline of categories, see Marie L. Radford, "Relational Aspects of Reference Interactions: A Qualitative Investigation of the Perceptions of Users and Librarians in the Academic Library" (Ph.D. diss., Rutgers—State Univ. of New Jersey, 1993).

6. The multichromatic analysis technique was developed by de Chesnay and

described by Edwina Skiba-King, "An Examination of the Patterns of Self-Reported Disclosure by Incest Survivors" (Ph.D. diss., Rutgers—State Univ. of New Jersey, 1993). For a fuller description of this technique, see Radford, "Relational Aspects of Reference Interactions."

7. See appendix G.

8. All quotations are taken verbatim from the librarian–user interview transcripts, unless otherwise noted.

9. See appendix G.

10. See appendix G.

11. See appendix G.

Chapter 6

Critical Incident Technique: Analysis and Results

❧ ❧ ❧ ❧ ❧ ❧ ❧ ❧ ❧

*T*he critical incident technique, developed by John C. Flanagan, has been used extensively in a variety of fields, including library science and communication.[1] This qualitative method puts forth a "flexible set of principles" that allow interview data to be sorted into patterns or relationships, and then summarized and described effectively. A *critical incident* is defined as "any observable human activity that is sufficiently complete in itself to permit inferences and predictions to be made about the persons performing the act."[2] For an incident to be judged as critical, it:

> must occur in a situation where the purpose or intent of the act seems fairly clear to the observer and where its consequences are sufficiently definite to leave little doubt concerning its effects.[3]

Establishing the aim or goal of the activity is thus necessary in using the critical incident technique. After the interview data are obtained, as described below, the collected incidents are sorted into categories and classified. This step is difficult, "inductive and relatively subjective,"[4] and has caused debate among researchers, as noted by Bengt-Erik Andersson and Stig-Goran Nilsson:

> It is clear that different people may systematize incidents in different ways. But one can always refer to the source material. The

essential thing seems therefore to be that the category system chosen is an obvious one, and with as small a degree of arbitrariness and chance as possible.[5]

However, according to Flanagan:

Once a classification system has been developed for any given type of critical incidents, a fairly satisfactory degree of objectivity can be achieved in placing the incidents in the defined categories.[6]

Use of the Critical Incident Technique

In the library reference setting, the critical incident technique involves asking librarians and users to describe successful and unsuccessful reference interactions and to give their reasons for categorizing them as such. This technique allowed analysis to focus precisely on research questions three and four:

• What aspects of the relational dimensions of communication are judged to be of critical importance by librarians and library users in reference encounters?

• Do those aspects of relational dimensions of communication judged of critical importance by users differ from those of librarians, if and, so, how?

During the interviews, following the procedures of critical incident technique, each informant was asked to recall and describe:[7]

• a previous successful reference interaction;

• a previous unsuccessful reference interaction;

• the factors that made the interaction successful or unsuccessful.

Librarians and library users were asked to give their definitions of successful and unsuccessful. Rather than imposing standard definitions of success or failure, the analysis sought to identify the criteria used by the participants themselves in determining positive or negative perceptions. This approach is an integral part of the critical incident technique, which allows for:

the emergence—rather than the imposition—of an evaluative schema, and focus on the events and dimensions of the . . . experience which are most salient, memorable, and most likely to be retold to others.[8]

The critical incident technique is used to gather and analyze the most memorable experiences, not necessarily the most recent. As an exploratory method used to generate descriptions of various domains of study, the technique has been shown to be both reliable and valid, and appropriate for the description of communication processes.[9]

The author carefully and repeatedly read the interview transcripts to determine whether the informants perceived the incidents as successful or unsuccessful. Then she determined whether the crux of the success or failure of the interaction was associated with relational dimensions, content dimensions, or a combination of the two. The author underlined words and phrases that gave indications of these aspects in the transcript excerpts.

In so classifying the incidents, the author carefully considered and noted the emphasis (as inferred from repeated phrases or greater length of description) of the informant. She paid particular attention to answers to the question: What, for you, made the interaction successful or unsuccessful? Many times the informant would discuss both content and relational dimensions but would describe one in more detail. The author classified incidents as combination only if they discussed both content and relational aspects as contributing equally to perceptions of the success/failure of the interaction. If an incident included a discussion of both relational and content dimensions but was primarily weighted in one direction, the author placed it in the more heavily weighted one.

After placing the incidents into the major categories of content, relational, or combination, the researcher again analyzed them, this time with the aim of identifying the underlying themes. She developed a simplified coding scheme for identifying and classifying the critical incidents that used the major themes from the outline of categories, described in chapter 5.[10] Further, she modified the critical incident coding scheme during the course of analysis as new categories were found to be present and old ones were eliminated, changed, or combined with others. The final coding scheme contained three major content-related themes and five major relational themes with several subcategories. This coding scheme was also used in the analysis of paired perceptions described in chapter 7.

Critical Incident Coding Scheme and Explanation of Category Placement

Content Themes—Coding Scheme

The author categorized the critical incidents as content (C) if the user or librarian *primarily* discussed one or more of the following as associated with his or her perception of the success/failure of the interaction:

1. Information
   1.1 Information delivery/retrieval (or lack of) (e.g., information handed to user, directions provided to user, librarian acts as intermediary)
   1.2 Information access (or lack of)(*e.g.*, librarian arranged for user to gain entry to a restricted collection)
   1.3 Accuracy (or lack of) ability to find the "right answer"
   1.4 Product oriented (e.g., librarian or user concerned with finished product such as speech or paper, rather than with the process of research)
   1.5 Information technology

2. Knowledge base (or lack of knowledge base) (e.g., librarian provides specialized knowledge of library sources or systems)
   2.1 General knowledge
   2.2 Specialized knowledge
       2.21 Subject knowledge
       2.22 Knowledge of library science
       2.23 Knowledge about information need
       2.24 Knowledge of how to articulate need
       2.25 Knowledge of tools, information sources

Relational Themes—Coding Scheme

The author categorized the critical incidents as relational (R) if the librarian or user *primarily* discussed one or more of the following as associated with his or her perception of the success/failure of the interaction:

1. Attitude
   1.1 Attitude toward librarian or user
       1.11 Positive (e.g., supportive, friendly, helpful)
       1.12 Negative (e.g., angry, impatient, resisting)
   1.2 Attitude toward task
       1.21 Positive (e.g., persistent)
       1.22 Negative (e.g., uninterested)

2. Relationship quality
   2.1 Quality of communication skills
   2.2 Orientation toward process (e.g., librarian or user concerned primarily with teaching/learning the research process)
3. Approachability of librarian
   3.1 Positive nonverbal behavior (e.g., smiling, nodding)
   3.2 Negative nonverbal behavior (e.g., frowning, staring)
4. Impact of technology on relationship

The author categorized the critical incidents as combination (C/R) only if librarians and users discussed both content and relational dimensions as contributing equally to their perceptions of success/failure of the interaction.

Results of the Critical Incident Technique Analysis[11]

The informants contributed a total of forty-seven critical incidents, fourteen from the librarians and thirty-three from the users. Table 22 summarizes the type of critical incidents collected. Of the fourteen incidents collected from the librarians, six were about successful interactions and eight, unsuccessful.[12] Users reported nineteen positive and fourteen negative incidents.[13]

Relational and content dimensions were found to be associated with both unsuccessful and successful interactions for librarians and users. Thirty-five (74%) of the total of forty-seven incidents centered on issues of relationship rather than on those of content. Table 23 summarizes these findings.

Users reported incidents that were related to relational aspects with greater frequency than did librarians. As table 23 indicates, of the fourteen incidents reported by librarians, seven (50%) were content related and seven (50%) relational. In contrast, of the thirty-three incidents reported by users, five (15%) were content related and twenty-eight (85%) relational. Librar-

Table 22 Types of Critical Incidents			
	Librarians (N=9)*	Users (N=29)*	Librarians and Users
Successful	6 (43%)	19 (58%)	25 (53%)
Unsuccessful	8 (57%)	14 (42%)	22 (47%)
Total	14	33	47
*Includes main study participants only.			

Table 23 Summary of Critical Incident Analysis			
	Librarians (N=9)*	Users (N=29)*	Librarians and Users
Successful			
content	4 (67%)	3 (16%)	
relational	2 (33%)	16 (84%)	
total	6	19	
Unsuccessful			
content	3 (37%)	2 (14%)	
relational	5 (63%)	12 (86%)	
total	8	14	
Aggregate			
content	7 (50%)	5 (15%)	12 (26%)
relational	7 (50%)	28 (85%)	35 (74%)
Total	14	33	47

*Includes main study participants only.

ians did, however, attribute a greater number of unsuccessful incidents, five (63%) to relational dimensions compared to three (37%) to content dimensions. For the librarians, relational dimensions were of greater importance in their reports of unsuccessful interactions.

Representative content-oriented and relational-oriented statements from both librarians and users are given in tables 24 and 25.

Librarians' Critical Incident Themes
Four themes emerged from the librarians' fourteen critical incidents, two related primarily to content—information and knowledge base—and two —attitude and relationship quality—related to the relational dimension.[14] Table 26 summarizes these four themes.

Table 26 shows that the number one ranked theme for librarians was relational in nature, indicating that this dimension was important to librarians. However, overall, both dimensions were represented equally, with the emergence of seven relational themes (six attitude and one relationship quality) and seven content themes (four information and three knowledge

---

Table 24
Representative Content-Oriented Statements

Librarians about Users

"He goes, 'Yeah, I'm going to use *Applied Science and Technology.*'" (L06)

"This student came in this afternoon for the census tract." (L05)

"So I said, 'Well, I didn't know, but I would look it up.'" (L09)

Users about Librarians

"To tell me exactly what kind of subjects to look under."(U04)

"[He] directed me to the law books."(U07)

"I was looking, trying to get specific information." (U08)

Table 25
Representative Relational-Oriented Statements

Librarians about Users

"He was angry, he was angry when he started." (L01)

"A lot of it was his attitude."(L06)

"She kept interrupting each time." (L08)

"It was also exciting because she was very excited about the whole thing." (L06)

Users about Librarians

"She was very nice and helpful and pleasant. . . . She felt comfortable." (U08)

"She went out of her way." (U16)

"She treated me like she wanted to be treated herself, you know, with respect." (U19)

base). The discussion below describes these four themes with representative librarians' statements.

Attitude

User attitude was an important dimension for librarians. Attitude was the largest theme, relational in nature and evident in six (43%) out of fourteen incidents. Five out of the six incidents classified as relational were perceived as unsuccessful and attributed to users' poor attitude toward the librarian or toward the task. These centered on users who were perceived as:

- closed-minded;
- angry;
- arrogant;
- obnoxious;
- impatient.

Two quotes illustrate:

> He already had in his mind what he wanted me to produce, and I had a lot of trouble getting from him enough information to even look for what he wanted because he had a closed mind. (LU1)[15]

> And, you know, he kept saying, "Well, you . . . we've got to find this information" and I just couldn't produce it and he was very angry. He was angry when he started, he got angrier at me because I didn't seem to understand what it was he was trying to say, and I *did* understand what it was, it was just that I couldn't produce the information. (LU2)

Table 26			
Themes of Librarians' Critical Incidents			
Theme	**Responses**	**Percent**	**Rank**
Attitude	6 (5U,1S)	43	1 (R)
Information	4 (3U,1S)	29	2 (C)
Knowledge base	3 (3S)	21	3 (C)
Relationship quality	1 (S)	7	4 (R)
Total	14 (6S,8U)	100	
U= Unsuccessful C= Content S= Successful R= Relational			

Another incident involved a positive user attitude and openness. When asked what made this incident successful, the librarian replied: "I think her attitude. She was willing to explain those things [when] I asked her questions." (LS5)

Information

The second highest-ranked theme for librarians was information, with four (29%) of fourteen incidents.

Two unsuccessful incidents focused on the librarian's inability to get access to information that the user was seeking. For example:

> A lot of times, we don't have what they want. Like this student came in this afternoon for the census tract for, I think it was one town near Philadelphia and one town in Maryland, and we don't have it. Things like that are unsuccessful just because we didn't have what they wanted. (LU4)

The third unsuccessful incident in the information theme centered on lack of accuracy, the librarian's perceived failure to find the right answer, in this case, while the user was still present. Although the librarian eventually did find the answer, it was not until after the user had left the library:

> So I hopped onto the catalog, typed in the *Japanese Encyclopedia* and it wasn't there, and I was so unnerved by everything that was going on around me, I said, "We don't have that." And then about twenty minutes later, and she went away, everything calmed down, and I said, "Oh, this is ridiculous" that I didn't try different things and I went back on and truncated and immediately I found the *Japan Encyclopedia* and, I was sure that was the one that she wanted. (LU8)

One positive incident dealt with information retrieval systems:

> Using those three terms, we got over two hundred articles on *Psyclit* and I explained that she needs to check our holdings to make sure that [site] has the article she wants to get it here and just to browse

through. And sometimes that's basically how we start off exposing them to the realm of the literature and then trying to focus in a little bit but like letting them make the choices. (LS2)

Knowledge Base

Besides the one content-related successful incident focused on information, three centered on knowledge base.[16] To illustrate:

And she wasn't quite sure how to access some of the secondary literature. There are a couple of bibliographies she hadn't worked with, so going from "I need something of Alfleck's" to these are the bibliographies that you should be using and these are the kinds of materials that are available, we were able to really expand on what she wanted and she walked away with much more than she had originally asked for. (LS4)

Relationship Quality

One of the librarians' incidents dealt with relationship quality. This theme is defined as the interpersonal dynamics of the interaction, such as perceptions of the other's communication skills and involvement in the reference process (i.e., willingness to invest time). One example follows:

I think it was because it took us a while before we really got to the point of what he really needed to know and then, I think, probably above and beyond the interview was the fact that I saw a kid's light bulb go on, and he really responded and you just knew that instead of this being a drudge now was, the paper, was gonna be fun and that was great to see . . . finally we got to what he really needed to know and then it was like it grew and it was almost like a flower, kind of. (LS1)

Users' Critical Incident Themes

The twenty-nine users reported thirty-three critical incidents. The author sorted these into the same four themes as the librarians' incidents, plus one additional theme—approachability (see table 27). A notable finding can be observed by comparing table 27 with table 26. Table 27 indicates that the theme ranked first for users was relational and involved positive or negative attitude. This was also the case for librarians as reported in table 26.

Attitude

Users reported a total of fourteen unsuccessful incidents. Twelve were classified as primarily relational. Six of these, similar to the librarians', were attributed to users' perceptions of negative librarian attitude described as:

- having no time;
- unhelpful;
- uncaring;
- sour;
- abrupt;
- impatient.

As an illustration, one user stated: "Yeah, well, some librarians are really sour and they're like 'Well, why don't you do your own research?' That kind of thing." (UU6) Another user commented: "And they're not very patient, they're, you know, 'Oh well, go to the computer.'" (UU9)

The users also reported nineteen successful interactions, sixteen primarily relational. Thirteen of these focused on attitude, more specifically on positive librarian attitude toward the user. Two representative excerpts follow:

> It's her normal job to help you get books, interlibrary loan, but there's no reason for her to have to stay late to do it and she didn't give me a hard time about it. She was interested more in helping me than in getting home. (US14)

Table 27			
Themes of Users' Critical Incidents			
Theme	**Responses**	**Percent**	**Rank**
Attitude	19 (6U,13S)	58	1 (R)
Relationship quality	7 (4U,3S)	21	2 (R)
Information	3 (S)	9	3 (C)
Approachability	2 (U)	6	4 (R)
Knowledge base	2 (U)	6	4 (C)
Total	33 (19S,14U)	100	
U= Unsuccessful　C= Content　S= Successful　R= Relational			

What stands out, I guess, for me is just, you know, getting involved, showing that, not that you're wholly enthused, but at least that you care, you're not just there. And I mean, there's some librarians, I guess, that don't want to be librarians and ... they're cold with you ... but like some that I've experienced, basically, they show that they're interested to help, not just feel that they have to. (US19)

Relationship Quality

Seven of the users' critical incidents were categorized as pertaining to relationship quality. Four of these were unsuccessful, as illustrated:

My first semester here, like it was my first time in the library, I asked for help. She says, "Oh, are you a freshman?" like that was expected, you know, that I needed her whatever, so she showed me where some things were, and then I came back and she goes "Well, didn't I just show you where it was?" And I was like "Yeah," I said, "but I think you just left me there, what was I supposed to do?" So I just, I think maybe that first time, like in a new library, very, not very nice. (UU8)

Three successful incidents also dealt with the relationship quality, as this example of a user essentially concerned with the teaching/learning process illustrates:

She really took the time to show me. She went out of her way then to show me so that maybe next time I could be more independent. (US11)

Information

Three of the users' successful incidents were primarily content related, concerned with information as represented by this passage:

I think it was giving me the book, opening it up and telling me this is what you want, this is what you need, and to tell me exactly what kind of subject to look under and not something vague [but] something really specific ... and that's what made it so successful. (US2)

Approachability

Approachability emerged for two users but was not present among the librarian themes. It dealt with users' perceptions of the librarian's nonverbal behaviors. Because the users were faced with the responsibility to approach the librarian, it was reasonable that they would be concerned with these perceptions. For example, this user commented on a librarian's lack of approachability:

> When they are not getting up from their desk or, you know, you can see that they are not happy to look for something for you really. (UU10)

Knowledge Base

The author classified two of the users' unsuccessful incidents as primarily content oriented, centering on perceptions that librarians lacked specialized knowledge. For example, one user asserted: "If the librarian doesn't know about it, then she can't really help you with it." (UU3)

Comparison of Librarian and User Themes

Table 28 summarizes the findings of user and librarian critical incidents. This analysis demonstrates the importance of the relational dimensions of communication, especially to users. When user and librarian responses are combined, the top two ranked themes are relational in nature, dealing with issues of attitude and relationship quality.

Table 29 presents the same information as table 28 but compares relational and content themes. This table shows that when librarians' and users' results were taken separately, attitude, a relational category, remains

---

Table 28
Themes of Critical Incidents of Users and Librarians

Theme	Responses	Percent	Rank
Attitude	25 (19U, 6L)	53	1 (R)
Relationship quality	8 (7U, 1L)	17	2 (R)
Information	7 (3U, 4L)	15	3 (C)
Knowledge base	5 (2U, 3L)	11	4 (C)
Approachability	2 (2U)	4	5 (R)
Total	47 (33U, 14L)	100	

U= Unsuccessful   C= Content   S= Successful   R= Relational

Table 29
Comparison of Librarians' and Users' Relational and
Content Critical Incident Themes

Theme	Librarians			Users		
	No.	%	Rank	No.	%	Rank
Relational						
Attitude	6	43	1	19	58	1
Relationship quality	1	7	4	7	21	2
Approachability	0			2	6	4
Content						
Information	4	29	2	3	9	3
Knowledge base	3	21	3	2	6	4
Total	14			33		

the number one–ranked theme for both users and librarians. However, relationship quality, ranked second for users, is ranked fourth for librarians. The content categories of information and knowledge base ranked higher for librarians.

Reliability Test
After the critical incidents were sorted into categories, twenty-four (51%) were sent to two additional judges for reliability tests. The author gave the judges verbatim transcripts, two model incidents with explanation as to how the categories were determined, the coding scheme, and instructions to follow in assigning categories. In one case, both judges disagreed with the author, who then changed her overall categorization of the incident and coding scheme assignment. After this, on the sort of incidents into relational, content, or combination categories, the judges had an average of 87 percent agreement with the author. Regarding the coding scheme themes, the judges had an average of 81 percent agreement with the author. The author believes that these levels of agreement are adequate.[17]

Discussion
The critical incident analysis shows that relational dimensions are important to users' and librarians' perceptions of the quality of reference interactions. Users reported incidents centering on relational aspects with greater fre-

quency than did librarians. On the other hand, librarians gave more weight to content dimensions, but they also perceived relationship qualities to be important. In fact, librarians attributed more unsuccessful incidents to relational dimensions than to content dimensions. Librarians tended to recall unsuccessful incidents in which the users were perceived as displaying negative relational messages, such as being nasty or obnoxious, rather than those in which the information exchange was incomplete or inaccurate. The emphasis on transfer of content in the literature on the reference interaction leads one to expect that librarians would attribute failure to unsuccessful information transfer. However, the critical incidents analysis shows that relational dimensions are also important. Additional discussion of these findings is provided in chapter 8.

Notes

1. John C. Flanagan, "The Critical Incident Technique," *Psychological Bulletin* 51 (July 1954): 327–58; see also Grace Fivars, *The Critical Incident Technique: A Bibliography* 2nd ed. (Palo Alto, Calif.: American Institutes for Research in the Behavioral Sciences, 1980).ERIC Document 195 681; Brent D. Ruben, "The Health Caregiver–Patient Relationship: Pathology, Etiology, Treatment," in *Communication and Health: Systems Perspective*, ed. Eileen B. Ray and Lewis Donohew (Hillsdale, N.J.: L. Erlbaum Associates, 1990), 51–68, Brent D. Ruben. *Communicating with Patients* (Dubuque, Ia.: Kendall-Hunt, 1992); ———, "What Patients Remember: A Content Analysis of Critical Incidents in Health Care," *Health Communication* 5 (1993): 1–16.

2. Flanagan, "The Critical Incident Technique," 327.

3. Ibid., 327.

4. Ibid., 335.

5. Bengt-Erik Andersson and Stig-Goran Nilsson, "Studies in the Reliability and Validity of the Critical Incident Technique," *Journal of Applied Psychology* 48 (1964): 400.

6. Flanagan, "The Critical Incident Technique," 335.

7. See appendix F. It should also be noted that the critical incidents elicited from users and librarians were, with the exception of two cases, unrelated to the observed interactions. The two exceptions, when asked to describe a successful interaction, spoke about the one that had just taken place.

8. Ruben, "What Patients Remember," 3.

9. See Andersson and Nilsson, "Studies in the Reliability and Validity of the Critical Incident Technique." and Lorette K. Woolsey, "The Critical Incident Technique: An Innovative Qualitative Method of Research," *Canadian Journal of Counseling* 20 (Oct. 1986): 242-54.

10. See appendix G.

11. Parts of this chapter were published in Marie L. Radford, "Communication Theory Applied to the Reference Encounter: An Analysis of Critical Incidents," *Library Quarterly* 66 (Apr. 1996): 123–37, and are reproduced here with permission.

12. Three librarians were unable to recall usable successful or unsuccessful incidents; one could not recall a successful incident. One librarian was able to recall two successful and two unsuccessful incidents, and another was able to recall two unsuccessful incidents, which were deemed usable.

13. Two users were unable to recall usable successful or unsuccessful incidents, five were unable to recall usable successful incidents, and ten were unable to recall unsuccessful incidents. Due to time pressure, one user was unable to complete the interview and therefore did not report critical incidents.

14. See chapter 5 for definitions of *attitude, information,* and *knowledge base.*

15. The notation "LU1" stands for librarian, unsuccessful, critical incident number 1. "LS1" would stand for librarian, successful, critical incident number 1. Likewise, "UU" would stand for user, unsuccessful, critical incident number 1 and "US1" for user, successful, critical incident number 1.

16. See chapter 5 for a definition of *knowledge base.*

17. For a more detailed description of the reliability test, see Marie L. Radford, "Relational Aspects of Reference Interactions: A Qualitative Investigation of the Perceptions of Users and Librarians in the Academic Library" (Ph.D. diss., Rutgers—State Univ. of New Jersey, 1993), 157–59.

Chapter 7

Paired Perceptions: Analysis and Results

❦❧ ❦❧ ❦❧ ❦❧ ❦❧ ❦❧ ❦❧ ❦❧ ❦❧

Although there have been quantitative surveys of librarian–user pairs, this book reports the first qualitative analysis of dual interviews, in which the author asked both user and librarian to talk about the same reference interaction right after it took place. The author developed this method of analysis to allow assessment of the extent of librarian–user agreement. The analysis aimed to answer the fourth research question: Do those aspects of relational dimensions of communication judged of critical importance by users differ from those of librarians, and if so, how? The analysis provided an additional insight into the qualities affecting the participants' perceptions of success and failure. The researcher especially noted areas of consonance or dissonance between user and librarian views of the same interaction. Also, she investigated perceptions pertaining to relational dimensions of communication and their relationship to the transfer of information. During each interview, the author asked informants to:

• recall and describe the reference interaction that just occurred;
• discuss how they thought the interaction went;
• recall and describe the factors that were important to them in the interaction;
• discuss whether they (users only) received the help they wanted.

Perceptions of Individual Participants
The first task was to determine if each individual participant perceived the

interaction to be successful, unsuccessful, or a combination of the two. The author did not determine success and failure by preexisting definitions but, rather, inferred them from the participants' responses to interview questions such as How do you think it went? Each transcript was examined carefully, and the author identified words or phrases indicating perceptions of success or failure. She then recorded these on work sheets. If the interactant reported positive perceptions, the author classified the interaction as successful, unsuccessful if negative perceptions were reported. The interactions classified as combination had some element perceived as successful (usually positive relational factors, e.g., librarian was helpful or patient), but another element perceived as unsuccessful (e.g., information was unavailable). The researcher analyzed each of the transcripts independently but recorded the analyses for the librarian and user pairs in parallel columns on the same work sheet.

Following this, the author further analyzed the transcripts to determine whether success or failure was attributed by the interactants to relational factors, content factors, or a combination. She again employed the coding scheme used in the critical incidents analysis to identify themes (see chapter 6). Words or phrases from the paired transcripts that gave indications of content or relational factors were identified and transferred to the work sheets. The author identified and recorded themes and underlying categories from these relational, content, or combination statements.

Extent of Pair Agreement

Through additional analysis, the author determined the extent of agreement of pairs of users and librarians about the success or failure of the interaction and its content/relational themes. Work sheets that provided side-by-side analysis of the users' and librarians' perceptions facilitated this analysis. If the pair agreed on the (1) assessment of success or failure of the interaction and (2) type of dimension (content or relational) to which they attributed that success or failure, the author classified the pair as being in total agreement. If the pair agreed on (1), but disagreed on (2) or disagreed on (1) but agreed on (2), the author classified the pair as being in partial agreement. If they disagreed on both (1) and (2), the author classified the pair as being in total disagreement. Examples of statements that illustrate these classifications are provided below.

Table 30
Summary of Paired Perceptions

	Librarians	Users	Librarians and Users
Successful	20 (74%)	25 (92%)	45 (83%)
Unsuccessful	3 (11%)	1 (4%)	4 (7%)
Combination	4 (15%)	1 (4%)	5 (9%)
Total	27	27*	54

*There were 29 users but 27 interactions.

Results of Paired Perceptions Analysis

Users and librarians perceived a large majority of interactions to be success-ful (see table 30). Out of fifty-four total reports (one by each librarian and user[s] for each of twenty-seven interactions), participants classified forty-five (83%) as successful, four (7%) as unsuccessful, and five (9%) as combi-nation. Users were less critical than librarians in their perceptions of success. According to the users, 92 percent of the interactions were successful, whereas librarians described 74 percent as successful. Users described one unsuc-cessful interaction and one combination. Librarians said three were unsuc-

Table 31
Representative Success-Oriented Statements

Librarians
"It went well." (L07)

"I think he got what he needed." (L01)

Users
"It was useful to me." (U18)

"He gave me the information I needed, and that's basically what I was looking for, the right answers." (U14)

"It was good . . . she was very helpful." (U07)

"She knew exactly what I was looking for and where the information was and how to show me how to get it." (U08)

cessful and four were combinations, a total of seven (26%) out of twenty-seven. Examples of successful, unsuccessful, and combination statements are given in tables 31, 32, and 33.

Table 34 summarizes the findings of the analysis of whether the success or failure was attributed to relational dimensions, content dimensions, or a combination. Users attributed the outcome to relational dimensions with greater frequency than did librarians. Librarians reported twenty (74%) content-related interactions out of twenty-seven, whereas users reported

---

Table 32
Representative Unsuccessful Statements

Librarians

"These things usually are, from my experience, often not successful ... [I] didn't find [the information] and didn't know where else to look." (L05)

"It was left unresolved, if you will, or unfinished. ... I wasn't very satisfied with this one." (L04)

"I was not happy with the reference interview." (L04)

User

"I felt like she couldn't help me on my subject." (U22)

Table 33
Representative Combination Statements

Librarians

"I don't have the sense that he was really dissatisfied ... I couldn't find anything ... he was patient, his expectations weren't enormously high." (L06)

"The interaction itself went well, but the unsuccessful thing, I think, was the outcome of it. I wish we had found some more information." (L03)

User

"We didn't find the book, we couldn't find any information on the topic, but she went out of her way to help me. Was very helpful." (U05)

Table 34 Analysis of the Dimensions Contributing to Successful and Unsuccessful Interactions					
Librarians			**Users**		
Successful			Successful		
content	17	(85%)	content	7	(28%)
relational	3	(15%)	relational	18	(72%)
Total	20		Total	25	
Unsuccessful			Unsuccessful		
content	3	(100%)	content	0	
relational	0		relational	1	(100%)
Total	3		Total	1	
Combination (C&R)	4		Combination (C&R)	1	
Subtotal			Subtotal		
content	20	(74%)	content	7	(26%)
relational	3	(11%)	relational	19	(70%)
combination	4	(15%)	combination	1	(4%)
Total	27		Total	27	
Librarians and Users					
content			27 (20L, 7U) (50%)		
relational			22 (3L, 19U) (41%)		
combination (C&R)			5 (4L, 1U) (9%)		
Total			54 (27L, 27U)		

only seven (28%). In the successful interactions, seventeen (85%) out of twenty librarians perceived the outcome to be content related, whereas eighteen (72%) out of twenty-five users described the outcome in relational terms. This finding shows that relational dimensions played a major role for users, and content dimensions dominated for librarians.

Librarians' Themes
The author further analyzed the interactions to determine the themes in the

participants' reports. For the librarians, the themes of information, relationship quality, and attitude were important along with a combination theme that had elements of attitude and information (see table 35).[1]

The author categorized the largest proportion of the reference interactions, twenty out of twenty-seven (74%), as belonging to the information theme. Two subcategories were present:

- information delivery/retrieval;
- information access.

Excerpts below illustrate these subcategories:

Information —Librarians
Information Delivery/Retrieval

I wanted to be sure that he had sufficient material that would help him with his paper . . . he had a list of probably 20 or 30 books. (L01/U02)

Once I saw the [computer] screen full of information, I felt that we had accomplished what we set out to do. (L03/U08)

She had an information need, basically, a research need, and it turned out that it was very easy for me to figure out what she needed and so it was like a piece of cake. (L04/U12)

Table 35
Themes of Librarians in Paired Perceptions of Interactions

Theme	Responses	Percent	Rank
Information	20 (17S/3U)	74	1 (C)
Combination (Attitude & Information)	4 (S/U)	15	2 (C/R)
Relationship quality	2 (2S)	7	3 (R)
Attitude	1 (S)	4	4 (R)
Total	27 (20S, 3U, 4S/U)	100	

S= Successful   C= Content   U= Unsuccessful   R= Relational

Information Access

I think that I gave him the appropriate . . . I was leading him to the sources that ultimately will answer his question. (L04/U14)

Attitude—Librarians

One interaction represented the attitude theme. In this case, when asked how one interaction went, the librarian replied:

I think it went well because, first of all, she had the time and she was interested in learning how to do it. . . . She was an apt student, too. . . . I thought she was an interesting and interested student in what she was doing and doing a good job at it. (L08/U13)

Combination—Librarians

The combination theme categorized interactions that contained elements of both attitude and information in equal proportions. Four (15%) of the twenty-seven interactions fell into this category. In some cases, the librarians reported success (classified to be in the relational category) because of the user's attitude, but failure (classified as content) because the information was not found. One librarian reported a successful interaction that was due to both relational and content factors. In this example, the librarian felt that the information provided was successful:

I knew they had the information with which to move forward, but then I wasn't sure they were going to be able to secure the magazine. . . . Later on, I asked to make sure they were succeeding in getting to the magazines and they said yes. (L04/U15)

However, the librarian felt uncomfortable with the interpersonal aspects because he was physically attracted to the user:

I was not happy with the reference interview . . . because I felt as though I was not expressing myself smoothly, you know. Usually I complete my sentences and have a coherent statement, whereas this time I was kind of garbling things a bit and maybe because, {clears throat} this is kind of embarrassing to confess, but it happens and maybe it would be interesting for your research. Let's say you're a heterosexual, which is what I am, and if you're attracted to the patron, it kind of throws you off sometimes because the hormones interfere with the job, {laugh} so I think that's what was happening . . . it interferes with your work . . . you can't help but be affected and distracted, you know. (L04/U15)

Relationship Quality—Librarians

The researcher categorized two interactions perceived as successful by librarians, into the theme relationship quality. In this example, the librarian has worked with the user before on continuing research and has established an ongoing, positive relationship. When asked how the interaction went, the librarian replied:

It went well. You know, it's fun to be working with somebody like that, [who], you know, has been putting in time and doing some serious work on their topic. . . . It's much more rewarding than those that come in at the last minute. (L07/U18)

Users' Themes

The four themes that emerged for the librarians were also present for users, although ranked differently. However, users had one additional theme—knowledge base. These are summarized in table 36.

Attitude—Users

The author found that twelve (44%) of the twenty-seven interactions were

Table 36
Themes of Users in Paired Perceptions of Interactions

Theme	Responses	Percent	Rank
Attitude	12 (11S,1U)	44	1 (R)
Relationship quality	7 (S)	26	2 (R)
Information	5 (S)	19	3 (C)
Knowledge base	2 (S)	7	4 (C)
Combination	1 (S/U)	4	5 (R/C)
Total	27 (25S, 1U, 1S/U)	100	

S= Successful   C= Content   U= Unsuccessful   R= Relational

relational in nature and focused on the users' perceptions of the librarians' attitude toward them. No other theme had as many. Users reported that eleven of the twelve were successful. For example, one user commented:

> I think it went well, better than usual . . . 'cause she actually took the time. Usually they're, you know, nasty or so, but they're, she was very nice, very understanding. (U13/L08)

One of the interactions classified in the attitude theme was unsuccessful. This user describes her perceptions of the librarian's attitude as follows:

> I felt like she couldn't help me on my subject. [It] isn't that she didn't know the answer, but I felt that she didn't want to. That's basically it, it sounded too complicated and . . . also she more or less said, "Oh, look it up in the thesaurus." She looked like she did not know what I was talking about, a blank stare and also almost like irritated. (U22/L08)

Relationship Quality—Users

The author sorted seven (26%) of the users' responses into the relationship quality theme, ranked second. For example, one user felt inadequate in coming to the librarian for help but found that the librarian structured their interaction so that he was comfortable:

> She was nice. . . . She didn't treat me like I was an idiot even though I, she knew I had no idea what I was talking about, so I didn't feel uncomfortable with her. She was good about it. (U20/L09)

Information—Users

The information theme was ranked first in the librarians' categories for the interaction (see table 37). However, users ranked information third with five (19%) interactions. The researcher identified two subcategories:

- information delivery/retrieval;
- information need.

These excerpts illustrate these subcategories:

Information Delivery/Retrieval

He showed me what to look for and what books to use. . . . He gave me the information I needed, and that's basically what I was looking for, the right answer. (U14/L04)

Librarian was helpful . . . in directing us in which way to go, in what to do with the computer . . . you know, it just had lots of great sources. (U03/L04)

Information Need

He explained everything to me that I needed to know, where the microfiche was and if I had any further questions, he could direct me to more detailed information. (U12/L04)

Knowledge Base—Users

An additional theme for the users was knowledge base. The author placed two (7%) of the interactions in this category in which users attributed success to the librarian's knowledge. For example, when asked what made the interaction successful, one user replied: "She knew exactly what I was looking for and . . . where the information was and how to show me how to get it. . . . She did the job." (U08/L03)

Combination—Users

The author classified one interaction as combination, because it was seen as partially successful and partially unsuccessful, and also because it contained both relational and content aspects. In this case, the user did not obtain the information that was needed but felt that the relationship with the librarian was positive: "We didn't find the book, we couldn't find any information on the topic, but she went out of her way to help me. Was very helpful." (U05/L06)

Comparison of User and Librarian Themes

Table 37 summarizes the themes of users and librarians. The top-ranked factor for librarians and users is information with twenty-five (46%) of the fifty-four total views of the interactions (twenty-seven interactions times two viewpoints).

Table 37
Themes of Users and Librarians in Paired Perceptions of Interactions

Theme	Responses	Percent	Rank
Information	25 (5U,20L)	46	1 (C)
Attitude	13 (12U,1L)	24	2 (R)
Relationship Quality	9 (7U,2L)	17	3 (R)
Combination (Attitude & Information)	5 (1U,4L)	9	4 (C/R)
Knowledge Base	2 (U)	4	5 (C)
Total	54 (27U, 27L)	100	

U=User   C= Content   L=Librarian   R= Relational

Information is content related and ranked first because the author classified twenty (74%) of the twenty-seven librarian interactions into this category. Attitude with thirteen (24%) and relationship quality with nine (17%) were ranked second and third overall.

Table 38 shows that the factors for librarians and users, when displayed side by side, indicate an inverted ranking: the themes ranked high for librarians, information and combination, are rated lowest for users. Themes ranked high for users, attitude and relationship quality, ranked lowest for librarians.

Table 38
Comparison of Librarians' and Users' Relational and Content Paired Perception Themes

Theme	Librarians			Users		
	No.	%	Rank	No.	%	Rank
Relational						
attitude	1	4	4	12	44	1
rel. qual.	2	7	3	7	26	2
Combination	4	15	2	1	4	5
Content						
information	20	74	1	5	19	3
know. base	0			2	7	4
Total	27			27		

Level of Pair Agreement

An additional analysis determined the agreement of users and librarians with regard to their perceptions of success and content/relational dimensions. The author found that the paired perceptions belonged in one of three categories: total agreement, partial agreement, or total disagreement. In the case of both total agreement and partial agreement, both librarians and users indicated that all of the interactions were successful.

Pairs were in total agreement or partial agreement for twenty-one (78%) out of twenty-seven interactions which is noteworthy. However, librarians and users disagreed in ten of these cases, categorized as partial agreement, as to the reason for the success of the encounter. In nine of these, librarians were satisfied because of an emphasis on content factors and users were satisfied because of relational factors. Table 39 summarizes the level of agreement.

Table 39	
Summary of Level of Agreement for Paired Perceptions	
Total agreement (User–Successful, Librarian–Successful)	
User–content; librarian–content	7
User–relational; librarian–relational	3
User–combination, librarian–combination	1
Subtotal	11 (41%)
Partial agreement (User–Successful, Librarian–Successful)	
User–relational; librarian–content	9
User–relational; librarian–combination	1
Subtotal	10 (37%)
Total disagreement	
User–S, relational; librarian–U, content	3
User–U, relational; librarian–S, content	1
User–S, relational; librarian–combination, combination	2
Subtotal	6 (22%)
Total	27
S=Successful U=Unsuccessful	

Total Agreement

A typical paired perception in which the pair agreed that the interaction was successful is illustrated below. Here, both members of the dyad attributed the success to content factors, the user to the librarian's knowledge base and the librarian to the successful information retrieval:

Interaction #08

User 08	Librarian L03
It went well. She knew exactly what I was looking for and . . . where the information was and how to show me how to get it. . . . She did the job . . . She gave me a lot of information, some of it obviously, I couldn't remember it all.	At first, I was getting a little nervous because business is not really one of my, expertise . . . then it was like all avalanched, probably he had way more than he ever hoped. . . . Once I saw the screen full of information, I felt that we had accomplished what we set out to do.

The excerpt below also illustrates an interaction in which the pair are in total agreement, again that the interaction was successful, this time due to relational factors. Both librarian and user discuss the positive attitude of the other as critical to this success.

Interaction #13

User U13	Librarian L08
I think it went well, better than usual . . . 'cause she actually took the time; usually they're, you know, nasty or so, but she was very nice, very understanding, you know, knowing I didn't know anything about the computer or anything like that, so she was very nice, very nice.	I think it went well because, first of all, she had the time and she was interested in learning how to do it. . . . She was an apt student, too . . . I thought she was an interesting and interested student in what she was doing and doing a good job at it.

Partial Agreement

In ten interactions, the pairs agreed that the interaction was successful but disagreed on the perceived factors that led to this assessment. For nine out of ten of these, the users attributed success to relational dimensions and the librarians to content dimensions. Below, an excerpt illustrates this type of partial agreement.

Interaction #20

User U20

It went fine. She didn't treat me like I was an idiot even though I, she knew I had no idea what I was talking about, so I didn't feel uncomfortable with her. She was good about it.

Librarian L09

I thought it went very well. I mean, I felt I got to the heart of it very quickly. I think they left satisfied. I think they're, he's trying to accomplish what he came here to do.

Total Disagreement

In three of the interactions, total disagreement centered on the user perceiving the interaction to be successful along primarily relational dimensions, whereas the librarian found the interaction to be unsuccessful and attributed the failure to content dimensions. For example, the user in one interaction did not find the information but was satisfied with the librarian's helpfulness. However, the librarian was unsatisfied because the information need was not fulfilled.

Interaction #16

User U16

He was very receptive. Yeah, I would look for him next time. Before, I tried somebody else and she was not very receptive. He refreshed me as to going about different sources.

Librarian L04

It was left unresolved, if you will, or unfinished. She has to follow it up. It might or might not work out, so I wasn't very satisfied with this one. Our resources here are limited basically.

Although this user did not find the information, she described the interaction as positive. She found the librarian to be receptive when she had previously felt rejected and also reported a positive benefit in having been "refreshed" about the sources. The librarian, on the other hand, focused on the lack of information delivery and so was unsatisfied.

In contrast, one user perceived an interaction to be unsuccessful because of the librarian's attitude, a relational theme, whereas the librarian felt the interaction was a success because the user had found what she wanted. This excerpt, which was also described in chapter 1, exemplifies a type of miscommunication. The librarian had decided that the user was confident and able to function independently, but the user wanted additional help and felt cheated.

Interaction #22

User U22

I felt like she couldn't help me on my subject. [It] isn't that she didn't know the answer but I felt that she didn't want to. That's basically it, it sounded too complicated and she couldn't . . . and also she more or less said, 'Oh, look it up in the thesaurus.' She looked like she did not know what I was talking about, a blank stare, and also almost like irritated.

Librarian L08

I think it went alright from my viewpoint because I didn't have to really interact too much. She seemed capable, she seemed to know what she was doing. I felt she had found what she wanted because she said she had what she needed. She seemed to be capable of handling it on her own.

These examples illustrate the comparisons that the author made in analysis between user and librarian accounts of the same reference interactions. The overall level of total agreement between eleven pairs of librarians and users (41%) is noteworthy, but there were ten pairs (37%) with partial agreement and six pairs (22%) who totally disagreed. The interviews showed that librarians and users can have different viewpoints and striking differences in their criteria for determining success.

Reliability Test

After the twenty-seven paired perceptions of interactions were sorted into categories, seven (26%) were sent to two additional judges for reliability tests. The author gave the judges verbatim transcripts for both user and librarian interviews for each of the seven interactions, making a total of fourteen interview excerpts. The author also gave them two model interactions with explanations as to how the categories were determined, the coding scheme, and detailed instructions to follow in assigning categories. In the categories of successful or unsuccessful, the judges had an average of 86% agreement with the author. In the categories of content or relational, the judges had an average of 82% agreement with the author (the author changed one content/relational categorization to agree with the judges.) Both judges commented that the transcripts were highly complex and that placement of some interactions into categories was difficult. The author believes that these levels of agreement are adequate.[2]

Discussion

The paired-perception analysis demonstrates that relational dimensions are vitally important to users in academic reference interactions. Librarians gave more weight than users to content dimensions in their assessments of success or failure but also perceived relationship qualities to be important. Users much more frequently reported that relational factors were critical to success in reference transactions than did librarians.

Further, most of the librarians made their assessments of success based on their perceptions of content dimensions: Was the answer to the user's query provided? This is in line with emphasis in the library literature and with the traditional information transfer model. Most users, however, based their judgments on their perceptions of the personal treatment they received. One implication of these findings is that librarians wishing to increase users' perceptions of success need to understand better both the relational dynamics of the reference interaction and their importance to users. Library users also would improve their interactions with librarians by better understanding these dynamics.

Data analysis revealed additional differences. Only eleven (41%) out of twenty-seven pairs were in total agreement about the factors that contributed to the success of the interaction. The remaining sixteen pairs disagreed over the aspects of the interaction that were important to success. The differences between the perceptions of librarians and users were also apparent in the interactions for which there is partial agreement or total disagreement. In the cases of partial agreement, nine out of ten users attributed success to relational dimensions, whereas librarians perceived this success to be attributed to content factors. In four of six cases of total disagreement, librarians' perceptions centered on content, whereas users focused on the relational dimensions.

Librarians in total disagreement with their partners tended to be more critical than users, making assessments of failure in three cases that users perceived to be successful. In these interactions, the information requested was not found, but the user found the interaction to be successful because of relational factors (such as the kindness of the librarian). Additional discussion of these findings is found in chapter 8.

Notes

1. See chapter five for definitions of the information, attitude, relationship quality, and knowledge base themes.

2. For a more detailed description of the reliability test, see Marie L. Radford, "Relational Aspects of Reference Interactions: A Qualitative Investigation of the Perceptions of Users and Librarians in the Academic Library" (Ph.D. diss., Rutgers—State Univ. of New Jersey, 1993), 180-81.

Chapter 8

Discussion of Findings

ဓာ ဓာ ဓာ ဓာ ဓာ ဓာ ဓာ ဓာ ဓာ

*T*he results reported in chapters 5, 6, and 7 demonstrate that a communication-centered approach to the reference encounter provides rich insights into the interpersonal dynamics between librarian and user not found in traditional librarian performance studies. Utilizing Paul Watzlawick, Janet H. Beavin, and Don D. Jackson's perspective enabled an exploration of this encounter in terms of its content and relational dimensions.[1] This chapter discusses the major and ancillary findings for each of the three analytical perspectives used in this study:
- the development of the outline of categories;
- the critical incident analysis;
- the analysis of paired perceptions.

The user–librarian interactions explored in this study revealed a high level of complexity. Even the simplest instance of human communication has an intricate structure, and the nature of the reference interview adds to this complexity.[2] Richard L. Street noted that in all types of interview situations:

> The question–answer sequence and power/status differences between participants impose greater constraints on interactants' verbal, vocal, and nonverbal behaviors than is often evident in conversational settings.[3]

Each of the perspectives for analyzing this study's data provided evidence of these constraints and accompanying complexity.

103

It is important to remember that this study recognizes the vital importance of providing accurate reference service. However, it did not seek to measure whether users received "the right answer" to their reference queries. Instead, the analysis sought to discover librarian–user perceptions of interactions and to identify the qualities that were critical in their evaluation of these interactions.

Major Findings

The major findings were as follows:

• Interpersonal relationships and communication are of great importance in librarian and user perceptions of reference interactions.

• Library users in academic settings place a high degree of significance on the attitude and personal qualities of the librarian giving reference assistance.

• Some users valued interpersonal aspects more than their receipt of information.

• Librarians were more likely than users to evaluate the reference encounter from content dimensions that involve the transfer of information.

• Librarians also perceive relationship qualities to be important in the success of reference interactions (although to a lesser degree than users).

The following section organizes and discusses the findings in relation to the study's four research questions.

Perceptions of Relational Dimensions

Research question 1 asked: What are the perceptions of the participants regarding the relational dimensions of communication between librarian and library user in the reference encounter?

The critical incident analysis found that relational factors were primary in thirty-five (74%) of the forty-seven positive and negative incidents. This finding emphasizes the importance of relational dimensions to both librarians and users in assessing reference interactions. For users, especially, relational dimensions determine success or failure in twenty-eight (85%) of thirty-three critical incidents (see chapter 6).

The large variety of relational themes developed in the outline of categories, as well as in the findings of the analysis of paired perceptions and critical incidents, suggested that there are multiple librarian–user perceptions regarding relational aspects. These deal with a wide range of emotional, affect-oriented dimensions. Some of these reveal basic emotional responses to perceptions of positive attitudes such as friendliness, honesty, patience, and respect, or negative attitudes such as fear, impatience, hostility, or insecurity. The full range of relational categories that emerged from the data are given under facilitators and barriers for both librarians and users. A few of these categories are explored to illustrate their complexity and to provide in-depth discussion of underlying relational aspects that may be present in reference interactions that can have a positive or negative impact on their outcome.

Honesty/Deception/Self-disclosure

One example of relational factors that have an impact on the interaction was positive perceptions of self-disclosure and openness or negative perceptions of deception or lack of self-disclosure. One librarian voiced an appreciation of two users for being open and forthright: "He was willing to reveal what the question was" (L06/U05) and "I think it went okay, I think she was up front about what it was that she wanted" (L06/U21). A related relational aspect is the user's willingness to trust the librarian. As one librarian said:

> I guess the willingness to trust the librarian, whether it be a confidential matter or just something that they weren't really comfortable talking about, because I think that's the whole problem with the reference interview—well, one of the problems—a lot of times the user comes up and doesn't really say what they want. Usually it starts out as a very general, broad subject, and then you find out they're really looking for a very specific piece of information. (L03)

The reason for such ambiguity or perhaps lack of self-disclosure by users was not known. At times, librarians perceived users to be ambiguous if they were unable to articulate their need. This was expressed by one librarian: "Maybe they don't have the ability to actually phrase the question" (L03). Another explanation might be that they are not aware of the precise nature of their information need.[4]

At other times, the user may have withheld some information or been deliberately deceptive. Several librarians speculated on these possibilities and discussed their negative impact on the reference interaction. In these cases, the user was perceived either to have been a surrogate, doing the research for another person,[5] or to have disguised the question for some reason, perhaps embarrassment or pretense. One librarian discussed instances when a form of surrogate user was encountered:

The most obvious one is the parent that actually will accompany the child. This usually happens in the public library environment, but due to the fact that this library does draw in a lot of the public, high school [students], I consider that perhaps a deception in the sense that the parent will speak on behalf of the child, even though I make it distinctly evident [by] my gestures . . . that I am trying to communicate with the person who will ultimately have to be the recipient of the knowledge and that sometimes the interaction is not winnable, and as such, I basically target the parent in the scenario as the person who is going to be on the receiving end of the knowledge that I am hopefully to impart. I guess that's a form of deception in a sense. (L02)

One of the most fascinating instances of deception involved a user who was perceived to be acting as a surrogate in researching background information for a take-home final examination for another student. The librarian commented:

Evidently, he must be doing it for a [this site] student because I know it's an assignment that's given here, it's a course that [this site] offers and I don't think that it's duplicated at his college. . . . I didn't ask him directly but I, just judging from what the other students who had this assignment did when they came in the library, which is *not* to approach us at *all*, they were all at the card catalog trying to work on their own . . . so it seemed to me that they had parameters that they were working with. And it's interesting that since we suspect that he might not have been working under those parameters, 'cause he's really the only one who came up and had like kinda in-depth conversation about this assignment. . . . I know a lot of students come in and sometimes when I ask them a few questions about their assignments, they say, "Oh I don't know. I'm doing it for someone else." So then I say, "It's not really helpful for them if you're doing it," but it happens. (L05)

Several indications suggested that this user was being deceptive. One was that he said he was a student at another college, but the librarian knew that the assignment was from a professor at the site. Also, he did not understand the assignment, whereas other students with the same assignment did not have this difficulty. Although this surrogacy/deception was suspected, the user did not admit it, nor did the librarian ask. Perhaps the user was deceptive because the assignment was a take-home exam in which seeking "help" with research might not have been acceptable. It was also noteworthy that the librarian had encountered "a lot" of students who admitted they were doing research for others.

Lack of self-disclosure was also related to privacy issues. For example, in the case of the user who was disguising the question because the topic was of a sensitive or personal nature:

The patron does not necessarily want to reveal the fact that he or she is preparing for a job interview and so the question will come . . . in a traditional company-specific question . . . or a search for statistics. But by a series of questions and the answers that the patron gives, it comes to the point that, yes indeed, the patron needs to secure information about a specific industry because he or she is preparing for an interview for a specific company. (L02)

Another librarian discussed the phenomenon of users asking questions that are disguised:

Sometimes people know what they want but ask for something else thinking that you know this is the question that they should be asking, and then they'll find what they want. I don't know . . . maybe they think their . . . own question is too revealing at first, I don't know, because I was reading an article in the *New York Times* about doctor–patient interactions and they said that the third question is usually the real question . . . and that the first two questions are sort of like feeling the ground and that doctors often don't even *get* to the third question and that was a problem. (L05)

Lack of self-disclosure and/or deception in reference interactions is an interesting relational aspect because it has a profound impact on the outcome of the interaction. Often a librarian is unable to help a user with an information need because the user may not be knowledgeable enough about the question to guide the librarian's efforts. In the case of a sensitive issue, the user may be deliberately withholding information that the librarian needs. Something similar can also happen in the case of the honest research assistant sent by a professor to find a piece of information in the library. The assistant does not have the specialized knowledge about the query that the professor would have. If it becomes necessary for the research assistant to interact with a librarian, he or she may be unable to explain or elaborate on the initial request. In such cases, the user creates an additional relational barrier that may prevent the librarian from understanding the user's need and thus preclude a successful outcome for the interaction.

Marilyn Markham, Keith H. Stirling, and Nathan M. Smith studied self-disclosure in the reference interaction, but they focused on the librarians.[6] They found that user comfort and satisfaction were positively affected by librarian self-disclosure, that "librarian self-disclosure was significantly correlated to the feeling that the interview was warm, friendly, and interesting."[7] They also found that there was more self-disclosure on the part of the user than the librarian.[8] Markham, Stirling, and Smith recommended additional research in this area and posed the following questions as possible research directions:

Why do patrons self-disclose more and how much more? Do they do so because they are in a position of weakness and uncertainty? Do they self-disclose in a subconscious effort to obtain self-disclosure and sympathy/warmth from the librarian? And perhaps the most fascinating question is, What effect does patron self-disclosure have on the librarian's perception of the patron/interview and on his own self-disclosure?[9]

Fear

Another illustration of relational dimensions is the barrier of fear. Users and librarians both perceived that users may approach the reference interview with some degree of fear. This may be generalized from a fear of the library or librarian as a representative of a depersonalized institution.[10] One student, when asked if he thought librarians were scary said, "Not librarians, I think the library is" (U20). One librarian said:

> The kid who comes here, in many instances, is the first person in their family ever to go away to school . . . and there's a lot of fear just of the institution, the place itself, and so they may be reticent and they're afraid they are going to show their inadequacies. (L01)

It was also possible, according to this librarian, that fear may have been due to a negative interaction with a librarian or with a stereotypical female authority figure in the user's past:

> It could be that they didn't have a very good relationship with other women in the past . . . in authority. It could be a principal, it could be a schoolteacher, it could be their mother, it could be anybody that they just see standing there. (L01)

Users and librarians both mentioned that the user may fear looking stupid or being a bother to the librarian.[11] One user commented: "first of all, like going in just asking makes me feel dumb" (U14). Alternatively, if users are acting as surrogates, or practicing deception, as discussed above, they may fear being discovered or unmasked. Erving Goffman's concept of the impression management and "face" is useful here. Goffman defines *face* as "the positive social value a person effectively claims for himself . . . an image of self delineated in terms of approved social attributes."[12]

Reference interactions generally seem to be very threatening to the user's "face." This provides one explanation for the fear users have expressed of looking stupid in the eyes of the librarian, or perhaps in the eyes of other students who may also be waiting for help at the reference desk. In the case of deception, using Goffman's terminology, the user has put forth the "line" that he or she is a student working on his or her own assignment. Therefore, the user fears being "in wrong face" if the truth is discovered and the line is found to be false. If the user is caught, "he is likely to feel ashamed and inferior."[13]

Users and librarians also reported that many students tend to procrastinate and come to the library to work on a class assignment shortly before it is due. For the student, this adds elements of stress and fear that the assignment will not be done on time. One typical user said: "I was worried that I wasn't gonna get this done by today, which [is when] I need it, [I] leave things for the last minute" (U19). As the semester of data collection progressed, the level of activity and stress at the reference desk increased. In response to this stress, librarians reported becoming more focused on quickly finding information that was available at the site. During the earlier parts of the semester, interlibrary loan and visits by users to other sites were possible, but by the end of the semester, the push was to get something into the users' hands immediately:

> What was important to me always at this point is that I help these kids find something 'cause they're feeling so desperate and I feel desperate if I haven't been able to come up with one or two pieces of something for them (L07/U17).

This librarian clearly had empathy for users' feelings of desperation and reacted with increased effort on the users' behalf. Similarly, understanding that users may be experiencing feelings of fear in approaching the reference interview may help librarians to work toward overcoming this barrier.

Attraction

One librarian described a barrier to success in an interaction in which he was physically attracted to the user. Here, a male librarian was attracted to a female student and felt that this interfered with his ability to answer the reference question:

The reason I guess I was not happy with the reference interview was because I felt as though I was not expressing myself smoothly, you know. Usually I complete my sentences and have a coherent statement, whereas this time I was kind of garbling things a bit and maybe because . . . {clears throat} this is kind of embarrassing to confess, but it happens and maybe it would be interesting for your research. Let's say you're a heterosexual, which is what I am, and if you're attracted to the patron, it kind of throws you off sometimes because the hormones interfere with the job {laugh} so I think that's what was happening . . . it interferes with your work . . . you can't help but be affected and distracted, you know. (L04)

When asked if he would changed anything if given the chance to go back and do it again, the librarian replied:

Well, if I could control my, you know, that eroticism, it would be better but, you know, we're human beings . . . you can't necessarily crush that, you know, [you] can only control it to a point, so . . . yeah, maybe I'm more disciplined, maybe when I grow a little older I'll slow down more, and it, and I'll be a better reference librarian because of that. (L04)

This was noteworthy because the researcher was unable to find any reference in the library literature to the effects of sexual or interpersonal attraction on the reference interaction. However, there is literature that explores this topic within other professions (e.g., therapist–client[14] and nurse–patient).[15]

This excerpt also gave evidence that a high level of trust was established between the researcher and informant. Because this was an obviously embarrassing and personal admission, the librarian must have had a sufficiently high level of trust to "confess," to use the librarian's word, these feelings. Also, this librarian had a high regard for the research being undertaken, as the informant said above: ". . . it happens and maybe it would be interesting for your research."

These examples of deception, fear, and attraction illustrate the range and complexity of the perceptions associated with relational dimensions in the librarian–user interaction. Heretofore, in the library literature issues of affect were rarely investigated empirically. This study demonstrates that affect has a major impact on the reference encounter.

Relative Importance of Relational versus Content Dimensions

Research question 2 asked: What is the relative importance of relational dimensions versus content dimensions of communication as perceived by librarian and library user in the reference encounter?

Relational dimensions were very important to library users in determining perceptions of success and failure in interactions. The outline of categories showed that users and librarians discussed relational concerns with greater frequency than content factors. However, analysis of paired perceptions and critical incidents found that librarians gave more weight to content dimensions in their assessment of success or failure of interactions. At the same time, those analyses showed that relational qualities were also important to librarians.

As mentioned previously, in the development of the category outline, three major themes were derived from the data:

- goals or aims of the interaction;
- facilitators: qualities that enhance goals, communication;
- barriers: characteristics that impede goals, communication.

Goals or aims of the interaction are important because the reference interview is considered to be goal-directed communication. Charles R. Berger and Patrick diBattista have noted that:

> Increasing numbers of interpersonal communication researchers have found it useful to view social interaction processes from a strategic, goal-directed perspective.[16]

To begin to understand the process, it was vital to consider the goals of the informants. The librarians and users both agreed that one goal of this type of interaction was to provide an exchange of information.[17] All were interested in solving an information problem or meeting an information need. However, the category outline had a fuller and more diversified range of goals for librarians than for the users. All of the librarians mentioned two or more goals for the interaction, whereas most users specified only one goal. Also, the librarians had additional goals that were not voiced by all users. These goals dealt with:

- *problem definition*, understanding the user's question;
- *enablement*, helping the user learn to become more independent in library use.

Nine librarians had problem definition as a goal, seven mentioned developing strategies for solving the problem and six discussed enablement. Only two librarians mentioned relational goals that dealt with gaining the user's confidence and developing positive attitude toward library program besides the information-oriented goals.

Users, by contrast, had one primary goal developing strategies for solving the problem. Only two users, both of whom were graduate students, reported the goal enablement. This suggests that, for the most part, users were not concerned with going beyond their immediate need to complete the assignment at hand. The data further showed that librarians were also interested in providing instruction so that the users could become more independent. One librarian commented on this:

> Somebody comes to the desk, they ask a question—well half of them are in a panic . . . they're not interested in the options, they're not really interested in learning how to use the library, they just want the quickest way in and the quickest way out. And even though I'm trying to squeeze in certain things, they're not absorbing it and it's a little frustrating. . . . If they had come in earlier and were more willing to put more into it, maybe they would be better off. (L09)

The conflict in goals was apparent here. It appeared that librarians were far more concerned with future library use and teaching the mechanics of the search process (note the reference to "trying to squeeze in certain things"). For comparison, the academic user wants to "find it [the information] quickly, as soon as possible so I can get done with it." (U15)

Users and librarians were not operating with the same goals in the interaction. If users and librarians do not understand each other's perspective with relation to goals, they are working at cross-purposes, which contributes to frustration on both sides. One user perceived that the librarian was unwilling to help:

Yeah, some librarians are really sour and they're like "Why don't you do your own research?" . . . Once I called up [county library] and I needed the definition of one lousy word, and she was like "Well, you know, I'm not doing your research for you." (U10)

Perhaps the librarians' goal of enablement was in conflict here with the user's search for information. If the goal was to instruct users on how to do their own research, the librarian may have felt he or she would be doing the student a disfavor by "doing the research for you." Some users find this frustrating because they feel that if they knew how to find the information, they would not ask for the librarian's help. Several users reported that they always tried to find the information themselves before approaching the reference librarian. A typical user commented:

I only ask a librarian for help when I cannot find it myself . . . when I'm stuck on a certain subject or a certain aspect of my subject, then I go and ask her. . . . If I know where it is, why should I bother her? I mean she's here only if I absolutely, necessarily need her. (U18)

Evidence, such as the above comment, shows that users are concerned with their self-esteem and also do not want to "bother" the librarian. Given this, it is also interesting to note the almost total absence of relational concerns in the goal statements of both librarians and users. This finding provided evidence that librarians were not fully conscious of the possibility that the users might have been concerned about the interpersonal components of the interaction. It also shows that users may not be aware that they may have relational goals in addition to the goal of obtaining information or may not be able to articulate these goals. Sample goals for librarians that exemplify relational concerns might be to establish a positive relationship with the user; or to have a successful interpersonal encounter.

An important finding in the development of the category outline was that although users and librarians agreed that information transfer was the goal of reference, both discussed relational factors with greater frequency and in more detail than content dimensions. This was true for both facilitators and barriers. Participants' perceptions of relational aspects greatly influenced the success or failure of the interaction. Although librarians and users perceived the interaction to center on solving an information need, interpersonal factors entered their evaluation of the outcome.

A major finding in the analysis of paired perceptions was that users, much more frequently than librarians, reported that relational concerns were critical to the success or failure of the interaction. Librarians discussed content themes in recounting twenty (74%) of twenty-seven interactions (see chapter 7). Among successful interactions, librarians described content aspects in seventeen (85%) of twenty. In contrast, for users, eighteen (72%) of twenty-five successful interactions were categorized as relational in nature. In short, users stressed relational aspects and librarians focused on content themes.

The critical incident analysis (chapter 6) also found that users described relationally centered incidents with greater frequency than did librarians. Twenty-eight (85%) of the users' thirty-three reports focused on relational themes compared to seven (50%) of the librarians' fourteen. However, among unsuccessful incidents, librarians attributed more to relational dimensions than to content dimensions (five to three). This was an important finding because it suggests that, in some circumstances at least, librarians can be affected significantly by relational factors.

Given traditional standards for reference, librarians would be expected to judge failure of interactions based on unsuccessful information transfer. Indeed, in the paired perceptions analysis, librarians focused more on content than relational dimensions. Instead, this finding of the critical incident analysis provides evidence that relational factors were important to librarians. An alternative explanation might be that librarians did not want to talk about interactions in which their reference skills were inadequate. Instead, they chose to speak of times when the user was at fault in being angry or uncooperative. The researcher considered this alternative, but it was also possible that these incidents were the first to come to the librarians' minds during the interviews or that memories that have a strong affective component may most easily be recalled. In any event, it appears that librarians retain their relational recollections, especially those that were unpleasant, longer than their content ones.

The analysis of paired perceptions revealed that librarians and users differed about the importance of relational versus content dimensions. Although forty-five (83%) of the fifty-four reports described the interactions as successful, only eleven (41%) out of twenty-seven pairs were in total agreement as to the factors that contributed to this success. The remaining sixteen librarian–user pairs disagreed about the aspects of the interaction that were important to success or failure.

The differences between the perceptions of librarians and users were either partial or total. In the category of partial agreement, in nine out of ten cases users attributed success to relational factors (most often related to the librarian's attitude or to relationship quality), whereas librarians credited success to content factors (most often related to information). In cases of total disagreement, librarians perceived four out of six cases to be centered on content whereas users focused on the relational.

Librarians in total disagreement with their user partners tended to be more negative about the interaction's outcome than users. Librarians assessed as failures three cases that users perceived to be successful. In these interactions, the information requested was not found, but the user perceived the interaction to be successful because of relational dimensions.

In contrast, librarians based their assessments of success on content factors alone, so "information not found equals failure." Only one user perceived an interaction to be unsuccessful. This user attributed the failure to relational components, not content. Benita J. Howell, Edward B. Reeves and John van Willigen similarly reported that librarians tended to rate their level of performance less favorably than did users.[18] Patricia Dewdney, in a study of users of public libraries, also found that users consistently rate service to be very high.[19] She offered one explanation for this: that users had little knowledge of the library and are impressed by the librarian's efforts regardless of effectiveness. Another, rather disturbing, explanation could be that users have low expectations for library service and so are pleased with any help they receive.[20]

The analysis of paired perceptions offered evidence that librarians concentrate more than users on content dimensions in the reference encounter. Invariably, each librarian told the researcher step by step the process and procedures used to find the information. Interpersonal aspects were discussed very briefly, if at all. Some librarians described the interaction in such detail (for example, the mechanics of a computer search) that the interviewer had to ask them to condense. To get any response from most of the librarians regarding relational factors, the researcher often had to ask probing questions such as How about the interpersonal aspects? A typical librarian's description of an interaction was as follows:

> Okay, he was looking for information on [x group] as I remember, but he wanted a very small, specific subsidiary which that name escapes me right now . . . but he knew that was a pretty recent subsidiary, so he wasn't sure how much information would be there. So I started looking our, through just our general reference books and I wasn't finding what we knew was, it was some kind of financial corporation, and they had just acquired [hotel chains]. So anyway, we were checking in *Moody's* and *Standard & Poors* and we were finding [x] entries but not [company x] *group,* so I started [getting] a little worried. So I came up to the ready reference area and looked in the *Million Dollar Directory* and one of the others, and we actually did find [it]. I just wanted to make sure that what we were looking for actually existed and it was under the right name. I . . . was trying to figure out whether it was a public or private company, it didn't have the little symbol for public. I was, I told him about *Compact Disclosure* which . . . is a CD-Rom product . . . but it would only be really for public companies. Well, during our whole process it was never actually free . . . then I decided that we should go into periodical literature and I was going to show him the {laugh} *Business Periodicals Index,* but I decided we could try *Infotrac* 'cause it seemed like it might have general information, but I didn't realize that they had loaded the *Business Index* on . . . to that machine, I was like "Oh, this is perfect," so he went in there, so it was like the business *Infotrac* and he found a lot. I think he found a lot of good information. He basically, wanted to just read up on, this was an interview-type thing, he just wanted to find out as much information as he could. . . . (L03)

This description continued for a few more paragraphs and exemplifies the level of specificity of some librarians' recollections. It also showed the attention given to the content dimension—in this case, the search for information. Possibly this librarian and others were attempting to demonstrate their expertise to the researcher by giving detailed explanations of their search strategy. In contrast, the user simply described the interaction:

> Well, I was looking for information on a company . . . trying to find out a little background on a particular company. . . . She helped me find a company reference which included employee information, gross sales. They recently acquired a couple of other companies so I was trying to find a little background, got into the periodicals. She showed me how the computer . . . to look up those references . . . showed me how to get to the periodicals after I found them {laugh}. (U08)

The user's very brief account is a far cry from the detail of the librarian. This user, atypically, did not get into the relational aspects of the interaction. Normally, users combined content with relational dimensions. For example:

> Well, she directed me to where I could find a reference book on the person that I'm looking for and she stayed with me a couple minutes and discussed, you know, how to go about looking for this person. *Unfortunately,* I couldn't find him. . . . Well, she tried to help as much as she could . . . you know, I felt comfortable with the what she was telling me. (U11)

User 11 gave a brief description of the content aspect of the interaction, but when asked how it went gave the relational information that "I felt comfortable." When prompted with the same question, librarians consistently gave their assessment of the quality of the information exchange.

Relational Dimensions Critical to Librarians and Library Users

Research question 3 asked: What aspects of the relational dimensions of communication are judged to be of critical importance by librarians and library users in reference encounters?

Three categories of relational dimensions emerged for users and librarians under the themes of facilitators and barriers:

- attitude;

- relationship quality;
- approachability.

These themes appeared to be vitally important in the analysis of the outline of categories, paired perceptions, and the critical incidents. Because the same informants provided the critical incidents as well as the paired perceptions, it is not surprising that similar elements would be present in their recollection and discussion.

In the category outline, under librarians' perceptions of positive user characteristics, relationship quality is more fully developed than attitude. The most critical factor in relationship quality appears to be user enthusiasm or interest, which was mentioned by eight librarians. Also important was good communication skills, especially the user's willingness to be open and direct. Under attitude, more librarians discussed the user's positive attitude toward task than the user's positive attitude toward librarian. Librarians described as important to users' success their being serious, motivated, assertive, and persistent. This description contrasted with users who gave greater emphasis to librarians having a positive attitude toward the user than having a positive attitude toward task. Perhaps users expected that the librarian would have a positive attitude toward their job but were more concerned about the librarian's attitude toward them.

In the critical incident analysis, attitude was the number one ranked theme for both users and librarians. This finding gave further weight to the importance of attitude. Relationship quality also rated high for users in their perceptions of success or failure. Similarly, in the paired perception analysis, users ranked attitude of librarian first with twelve (44%) out of twenty-seven interactions and relationship quality second with seven (26%). In contrast, librarians ranked attitude of users fourth, but rated first information, a content theme, (in twenty [74%] out of the twenty-seven interactions). A combination category of attitude and information ranked second with librarians.

Results from the critical incident and paired perception analyses suggest that attitude was most critical in users' perceptions of success or failure. Librarians, however, were more concerned with the content dimension of information or combinations of information exchange and user's attitude. It also may be that librarians made judgments primarily based on information transfer, but secondarily because of the relational factors.

Differences between Librarians and Users on Critical Relational Dimensions

Research question 4 asked: Do those aspects of relational dimensions of communication judged of critical importance by users differ from those of librarians, and if so, how?

It is clear that the evaluation criteria of librarians differed from those of users. Because librarians have traditionally learned to evaluate the success of the reference interaction based on the information exchange, it was not surprising that they tended to assess their interactions in terms of their ability to provide the correct information. The analysis of paired perceptions suggested that when information was unavailable or incomplete, librarians believed the interaction to be unsuccessful. Users, on the other hand, thought the interaction was successful if the librarian was pleasant and tried to help them, even if the information was not obtained. Often users do not possess the knowledge necessary to evaluate the librarian's technical performance, so they emphasize the interpersonal qualities.[21]

The Importance of Attitude

As noted above, in the critical incident analysis, the number one ranked factor for librarians and users is attitude. For librarians, six (43%) of fourteen incidents were categorized as attitude of user, five of these were negative, one positive. For users, nineteen (58%) out of thirty-three incidents were related to this theme, six negative and thirteen positive. In short for users and librarians the attitude of the other in the interaction was the most important relational aspect. Further, librarians were especially sensitive to negative user attitude toward themselves and toward the task.

Attitude was the only factor ranked similarly by librarians and users in the critical incident analysis. Following attitude, librarians ranked content dimensions information and knowledge base as second and third, and relationship quality, a relational theme, as fourth. Users, in contrast, ranked relationship quality second, making their two top-ranked categories relational, encompassing twenty-six out of thirty-three incidents. This finding makes a strong case for relational aspects being of overall greater importance to users than to librarians.

The relational theme of approachability emerged in two of the unsuccessful incidents for users, but not for librarians. Users were found to be more sensitive to librarians' nonverbal behavior than librarians were to users' nonverbal cues.

As seen in the outline of categories, both users and librarians discussed many relational qualities, but the librarians placed greater emphasis on the user's attitude toward task whereas users tended to emphasize the librarian's attitude toward user. Regarding facilitators, for the librarians, it may be more important that the user be interested and enthusiastic (mentioned by more librarians than any other quality). Users placed importance upon the librarian being helpful and nice.

Barriers

In the area of barriers, the librarians' category scheme dealing with content dimensions was more fully developed than that of users. Librarians emphasized lack of knowledge base as more critical to failure than did the users. Regarding relational barriers, the same subcategories emerged as did for facilitators:

- attitude;
- relationship quality;
- approachability (lack of).

For librarians, the number and diversity of subcategories under negative attitude toward librarian were more developed than negative attitude toward task, opposite the findings for facilitators, above. Most often, librarians reported that qualities in users such as impatient, fearful, and insecure were likely to lead to unsuccessful interactions. Thus, librarians perceived that a healthy user attitude toward task facilitated success, but a negative attitude toward librarian was more likely to lead to failure.

Both users and librarians reported that their negative perceptions were much more centered on relational factors. Under negative attitude of librarians, users' subcategories include evades user, resists user, and resists interaction. These were not present in the librarian's scheme. Perhaps this was because usually the user sought out the librarian for the interaction and so was more sensitive to perceptions that the librarian was trying to avoid contact. Evidence suggests that users perceived from the librarian's nonverbal behavior the librarian was resisting them or evading them. On the other hand, because users normally initiate the contact with librarians, librarians may not know which users are avoiding contact.

Several librarians described their frustration in laboring to help users, only to have their advice totally disregarded. These frustrations constitute the subcategory user rejecting librarian. One librarian commented:

The information that he was requesting was available in these particular sources, but he refused to even consider utilizing these particular sources (L02).

Another found this type of user behavior puzzling:

I don't know why they sometimes ask for something and then, you know, they practically throw it away as soon as you give it to them (L05).

This librarian may have felt personally rejected when the user discarded the proffered information.

Nonverbal Behaviors and Approachability

Overall, users were much more sensitive to librarians' nonverbal behaviors than librarians were to users'. Explicit references by librarians to users' nonverbal behavior were very infrequent. Regarding nonverbal behavior by librarians, a few librarians did discuss librarians' approachability. One librarian said good reference librarians needed to let the user know they were open and receptive. When probed about how this was communicated to the user, the librarian replied:

I think just when you're looking at them and nodding and 'cause I think I read something recently where it says people can be very intimidated if somebody's just sitting there silently while the person is explaining just kind of looking at them . . . It gets you nervous, it's like . . . they're not listening, they're just looking at me staring at me, they're not moving, they're not nodding . . . they don't look receptive at all. (L03)

Another librarian, when asked to describe qualities of a good reference librarian, mentioned the importance of being able to read nonverbal cues in the reference interview:

It's the ability to be able to read people, their gestures, their mannerisms, being able to assess psychological qualities that would allow a librarian to communicate better if indeed the librarian was not able to read these qualities. (L02)

Although librarians made few comments about nonverbal behavior, users were especially sensitive to the nonverbal behaviors of librarians. Users who may be approaching the reference librarian with some fear were more apt to be sensitive to the librarian's nonverbal cues. Perhaps they were looking for reassurance that their approach to the librarian was welcome. Four users mentioned negative affect when the librarian seemed distracted or inattentive. One user described this behavior:

Usually when they are not getting up from their desk or you can see that they are not happy to look for something for you really . . . It has happened a few times, usually they will just direct you to just go and look under such and such a journal . . . but they're not really making the effort. . . . Usually they will try to avoid some eye contact and just play like they're very busy and maybe they are. (U16)

Users were particularly aware of librarians' face and eye expression. The example above mentioned avoidance of eye contact, and another user, describing a negative interaction, said: "She looked like she did not know what I was talking about . . . a blank state and also almost like irritated." (U22) Users, sensitive to nonverbal behaviors, interpreted as negative actions those that librarians may think of as neutral behavior, such as having a cup of coffee at the reference desk or talking to another librarian.

The critical incident analysis also found two users but no librarians who reported that approachability affected the outcome of the interaction. This is further evidence that users were more sensitive to librarians' nonverbal behavior than librarians were to users' nonverbal cues. Findings of users' sensitivity to librarians' nonverbal behavior point out a need for librarians to become more conscious of the nonverbal behaviors they exhibit because these behaviors may be interpreted by users as barriers.[22]

Ancillary Findings: Time Pressure and Information Technologies

Time pressure was an external constraint perceived by librarians and users to be a barrier. In some cases, users need to leave the library in a short time, say, to be in class. Three students refused to be interviewed for this reason. Deadlines for assignments also create time pressure. These deadlines become more numerous as the semester draws to a close and users and librarians become increasingly stressed. Unlike many other professionals, librarians generally do not make appointments with library users. This ensures that at the busiest times of the semester, more users in need of urgent help actually got *less* of the librarian's time.[23] One librarian reported finishing with one user so she could return to the reference desk to help others:

> I was trying to get back to the desk, but I remember thinking when I left her there, I don't know if I noticed someone else was waiting or what, but I remember thinking when I left her at the *Negro Almanac* that I had to get back to the desk. (L05)

The librarian felt pressured to return to the reference desk, not sure that the user found the needed information in the almanac. One implication of these findings for practice is that at busy times more than one librarian should be on duty or available to relieve some of these time pressures. Librarians on duty alone could also ask users to return to the desk if additional help is needed. Finally, when busy times ease up, the librarian should check on users still at work.

Another impact of time constraints on reference interaction is the student's willingness to devote sufficient time to research. Students tend to procrastinate, waiting until deadlines loom, and want to do library work quickly. One librarian remembered a conversation with a user:

> "Oh there was an *excellent* article I just came upon, did you take that information?" . . . and she said, "Oh, no," she really "didn't have the time," so that was also frustrating if she did not really have the time to do it at that moment. (L08)

Users also seemed to be very conscious of the librarian's stinginess with their time. Three users described negative critical incidents in which they perceived the librarian as not being willing or able to spend enough time. One user commented:

> A few years back, I went in there looking for self-help books and the librarian was so busy, caught up in what she was doing, you know, she didn't have time to help everybody else.... She should have at least took the time out. She could get back to whatever she was doing, you know, at a later time. (U03)

Note that this encounter made a lasting impression on the user who remembered this busy librarian from "a few years back." Another user remarked that:

> It's like they have other things to do, don't have time for us. Yeah, you're taking out a book, they're sitting there and you're waiting for them, and they're like "Well *wait* a minute" and you're "Well, wait a minute, I have a class to go to, you're over here getting paid, you know, do something." (U15)

The time factor can also be a beneficial element. In one positive critical incident, the user was in a "time crunch" and was grateful that the librarian stayed a few minutes late to help with an interlibrary loan:

> I came in right at five o'clock when the interlibrary loan woman usually leaves, but she stayed a few extra minutes to help me get the forms so I could go and get the books. And I was in a time crunch, so I did need to get them right away. (U21)

Information Technology

There was little agreement among librarians about whether the new technologies were time-savers or time-wasters. One librarian discussed how electronic databases were faster than print:

> Probably, you know, if the computers are open, I always would try that as a first step because it takes more of my time to look in the print sources. If it's really busy, I'll say, "Sit down at that

computer and . . . try to play around with it and as soon as I get a chance, I'll come and help you with it." (L03)

One user also stated that information retrieval systems were time-savers: "Obviously the computer as a tool is just a big time-saver." (U08)

But some librarians believe that computerized information systems increased the time spent with each user. One librarian remarked that:

> The products were developed ultimately with hope that they would perhaps speed up or shorten the library user–librarian interaction, but it seems to have had, at least in this point in time, the opposite [effect] . . . per library user interview might have perhaps doubled in general.(L02)

This librarian also felt that the number of users needing help has risen but that "there are fewer members of the library staff" due to recent budget cuts. For this librarian, the "challenge is how to perhaps even just measure up to precomputer days." (L02)

Another librarian believed that, for the user, it was not an issue of using less time but, instead, getting more for the same amount of time used:

> It's more an issue of how much you're getting for your time, you know. The efficiency is really . . . what's happening is because of . . . this access to *more* information, the patron who is genuinely interested gets really excited and starts digging in much more than he or she might have if it was paper sources. . . . The patron may only have an hour . . . a lot of these students here, they work full-time and are doing the master's part-time. . . . Unfortunately, this is the reality. . . . so what is happening is that you're still spending the hour, but you're getting a lot more out of it because the technology is giving it to you faster. (L04)

Once again, this referred to the high premium on time—here, the user's. Also of interest is the librarian's reference to "efficiency."[24]

In addition to the disagreement on whether electronic resources save or cost time, there was also little agreement on the impact of information technologies on the nature of the reference interaction. Two librarians felt that the basic nature was unchanged. One commented:

> There's still a lot of work that is done by the librarian without the use of the technology so that there is still that interaction because, basically, you still have to find out what it is they want *before* you give them the technology. (L08)

In contrast, another librarian asserted that these technologies: "changed the entire interaction . . . from a skill perspective the interaction is more intensive . . . ."(L02) Several librarians felt that computerized information systems increased the librarian's involvement. One said:

> It's a lot more labor-intensive. . . . You're there a lot more, and they're calling on you a lot more. . . . They sort of think the librarian is the only source once they sit down in front of the computer. . . . They don't bother to read all the instructions . . . they just kind of turn around and want us to answer all their questions. . . . I think that makes the job a lot *different* . . . you're probably interacting more. (L05)

Another reflected on the effect of technologies on the user:

> I think it has brought some excitement and ease into the whole process. My favorite story was a lady, you know she hadn't been back to school for a while, she's probably in her mid-40s or whatever, and she's sitting over at the CD-ROM station giggling, and I walked over to her and I said, "You know, I really had to come over and find out {laugh} . . . I never heard anybody get quite this carried away." And she said, "This is so wonderful, I can't believe it. It's so much easier than it was before." And that comes in, you know, with the kids . . . creates a whole 'nother level in terms of, I think it's becoming more and more our role to help them learn to evaluate the information. (L07)

The librarian was referring to the fact that computerized databases provide such enormous amounts of information that the user has trouble deciding what is relevant. The idea that the librarian's role may be changing from information provider to include information evaluator is germane and challenges traditional conceptualizations in which librarians give out information but leave evaluation to the user.

Although librarians reported some users found computerized technology easy to use, one librarian perceived technology to be a barrier:

> Some patrons have computer phobia . . . have been threatened by it, feeling intimidated by it . . . so that does make a difference, but it's a minor factor because it's fairly easy to set them at ease. And if you feel that this is what's happening, you just spend a little more time with them at the computer. (L04)

This librarian was sensitive to users who feel threatened by technology. The librarian realized that attention to users' relational needs, by spending additional time to "set them at ease," was important to the success of the information retrieval. Susan Anthes has also discussed the need for "high touch," increased interpersonal involvement, between user and librarian as systems become increasingly complex.[25]

In summary, time constraints and information retrieval technologies had a great impact on the librarian–user interaction. The outline of categories lists the range of responses regarding these variables.[26] User and librarian informants both reported that these two factors are vitally important in understanding the present dynamics of the reference interaction.

Notes

1. Paul Watzlawick, Janet Helmick Beavin, and Don D. Jackson, *Pragmatics of Human Communication: A Study of Interactional Patterns, Pathologies, and Paradoxes.* (New York: Norton, 1967).

2. Helen Gothberg, "Immediacy: A Study of Communication Effect of the Reference Process," *Journal of Academic Librarianship* 2 (July 1976): 126–29.

3. Richard L. Street, "Interaction Processes and Outcomes in Interviews," in *Communication Yearbook* 9, ed. Margaret L. Mc Laughlin (Beverly Hills, Calif.: Sage, 1986), 215.

4. See also Nicholas J. Belkin, Robert N. Oddy, and Helen M. Brooks, "ASK for Information Retrieval, Part I: Background and Theory," *Journal of Documentation* 38 (June 1982): 61–71; ———, "ASK for Information Retrieval, Part II: Results of a Design Study," *Journal of Documentation* 38 (Sept. 1982): 145–64.

5. See also Melissa Gross, "The Imposed Query," *RQ* 35 (winter 1995): 236–43.

6. Marilyn Markham, Keith H. Stirling, and Nathan M. Smith, "Librarian Self-Disclosure and Patron Satisfaction in the Reference Interview," *RQ* 22 (summer 1983): 369–74.

7. Ibid., 373.

8. This was noted in chapter 2. See also Mark J. Thompson, Nathan M. Smith, and Bonnie L. Woods, "A Proposed Model of Self-Disclosure," *RQ* 20 (winter 1980): 160–64.

9. Markham, Stirling, and Smith, "Librarian Self-Disclosure and Paton Satisfaction in the Reference Interview," 373.

10. Michael E. Roloff, *Interpersonal Communication: The Social Exchange Approach.* (Beverly Hills, Calif.: Sage, 1981); see also Marie L. Radford and Gary P. Radford, "Power, Knowledge, and Fear: Feminism, Foucault and the Stereotype of the Female Librarian," *Library Quarterly* 67 (July 1997): 250–66.

11. Mary Jane Swope and Jeffrey Katzer, "Why Don't They Ask Questions?" *RQ* 12 (winter 1972): 161–66, had a similar finding in a study of academic library users.

12. Irving Goffman, *Interaction Ritual: Essays on Face-to-Face Behavior* (Garden City, N. Y.: Anchor, 1967), 5.

13. Ibid., 8.

14. See Jayne E. Stake and Joan Oliver, "Sexual Contact and Touching Between Therapist and Client—A Survey of Psychologist's Attitudes and Behavior," *Professional Psychology Research and Practice* 22 (Aug. 1991): 297–307.

15. See R. Gallop, "Interpersonal Attraction and Nursing Needs," *Nursing Papers: Perspectives in Nursing* 17 (1985): 30–40.

16. Charles R. Berger and Patrick diBattista, "Information Seeking and Plan Elaboration: What Do You Need to Know to Know What to Do?" *Communication Monographs* 59 (Dec. 1992), 368.

17. See also Street, "Interaction Processes and Outcomes in Interviews," who noted that the purpose of all types of interviews was to exchange information.

18. Benita J. Howell, Edward B. Reeves, and John van Willigen, "Fleeting Encounters—A Role Analysis of Reference Librarians–Patron Interaction," *RQ* 16 (winter 1976).

19. Patricia Dewdney, "The Effects of Training Reference Librarians in Interview Skills: A Field Experiment" (Ph.D. diss., School of Library and Information Service, Univ. of Western Ontario, 1986).

20. Janine Schmidt, "Evaluation of Reference Service in College Libraries in New South Wales, Australia," in *Library Effectiveness: A State of the Art*, comp. Neal K. Kaske and William G. Jones (Chicago: ALA, 1980), 265–89.

21. Brent D. Ruben, "What Patients Remember: A Content Analysis of Critical Incidents in Health Care," *Health Communication* 5 (1993): 1–16, reported a similar finding in a study of doctor–patient communication.

22. See also Marie L. Radford, "A Qualitative Investigation of Nonverbal Immediacy in the User's Decision to Approach the Academic Reference Librarian,"

presented at the Library Research Seminar I, Florida State Univ., Tallahassee, Fla., Nov. 1–2, 1996.

23. Thomas Lee Eichman, "The Complex Nature of Opening Reference Questions," *RQ* 17 (1978).

24. See also Jody Newmyer, "The Image Problem of the Librarian: Femininity and Social Control," *Journal of Library History* 11 (Jan. 1976): 44–67; Radford and Radford, "Power, Knowledge, and Fear"; Abigail A. Van Slyck, *Free to All: Carnegie Libraries and American Culture 1890–1920.* (Chicago: Univ. of Chicago Pr., 1995), for discussions of the origins of the stereotype of the librarian's preoccupation with efficiency.

25. Susan Anthes, "High Tech/High Touch: Academic Libraries Respond to Change in the Behavioral Sciences," *Behavioral & Social Sciences Librarian* 5 (fall 1985): 53–65.

26. See appendix G.

Chapter 9

Implications and
Future Directions

છે: છે: છે: છે: છે: છે: છે: છે: છે:

*T*his book presents the first thoroughly documented investigation of the relational dimensions of the interpersonal aspects of reference interactions. It shows that relational communication theory provides a powerful basis for analysis of this interaction and enables research to focus on important issues such as status differences, control, and context. Since Dervin's article on the application of communication theory to library scholarship, research efforts in this area have begun to develop.[1] Nevertheless, the application of communication theory to interpersonal encounters in the library context is still at the exploratory stage. This research demonstrates the value of its continued application.

Theoretical Implications

One major criticism of library research has been its lack of application of theoretical foundations. This study applies the heuristically rich relational theory from the communication field. Also, inclusion of the user's point of view in this study adds a piece that is missing in much research in the library field. This research demonstrates the importance of differentiating the viewpoints of users and librarians. Future research programs on the reference interaction should include the user's perspective.

Current conceptions of interpersonal communication have moved away from the static, information transmission, linear model expressed by some of this study's librarian informants. The linear model is usually represented as:

$$S \longrightarrow M \longrightarrow R$$

in which the sender (S) sends a message (M) to the receiver (R) with the meaning implicitly centered in the sender.[2] One librarian revealed this view of communication in the following comment:

> I am trying to communicate with the person who will ultimately have to be the recipient of the knowledge . . . . I basically target the parent in the scenario as the person who is going to be on the receiving end of the knowledge that I am hopefully to impart . . . (L02)

Process-oriented models of communication, emphasizing meaning and receiver interpretation, are replacing these information transfer, linear conceptualizations.[3] Evidence here argues for a new model of the librarian–user reference interaction. This new model recognizes the vital importance of the interpersonal, relational messages that are communicated in the encounter along with the information transferred. John V. Richardson Jr. believes that it is possible to have a "complete, balanced perspective" that incorporates knowledge of reference sources, the question negotiation process, and an understanding of the librarian–user interaction.[4] He asserts: "Perhaps only then will the field have reference librarians trained, educated, and capable of rendering high quality reference service."[5] This new model would also integrate both the user's and the librarian's perspective. Much more needs to be discovered before this model can be fully articulated.

There are other theoretical areas in communication, sociology, and related disciplines that would be useful to the study of librarian–user interactions. One of these is sociologist Erving Goffman's theory of impression management.[6] Impression management is a dramaturgical model that regards people as being concerned with managing the impressions that they present to others. Impression management consists of any behavior by a person that has the purpose of controlling or manipulating the attributions and impressions formed of that person by others.[7]

Many applications of the concepts of impression management have been made especially in psychological and sociological research.[8] A recent doctoral dissertation by Mary K. Chelton uses Goffman's theoretical basis in a study of the adult–adolescent service encounters in school libraries.[9]

Application of social exchange theory might also prove fruitful because some users approach the reference desk with conflicting desires and fears.[10] Social exchange theory holds that "relationships are sustained when they are relatively rewarding and discontinued when they are relatively costly."[11] Users need help with their library research, so they have to balance rewards (information) against possible costs (such as embarrassment, loss of face, or rejection).

Another area involves theories of interpersonal attraction. The analysis of paired perceptions described an encounter in which the librarian was sexually attracted to the user. Effects of interpersonal attraction on the reference interaction have not been explored in the library literature. There is a large body of attraction literature in the communication field that could apply.[12] These theories also address nonsexual interpersonal attraction that may help librarians appear more approachable to users.[13]

Future Directions

In addition to pursuing other theoretical approaches, another possible avenue for future research would be to replicate this study in other library contexts. Because this research was conducted at academic libraries, other types of libraries such as special, public, and school could be studied to see if results are similar. Librarian informants who have held positions in a variety of settings have suggested that special libraries, in particular, may yield results different from these. One librarian said: "In my experience, special library clients are less concerned with how they are treated, they are more focused on the bottom line."

Two of this study's ancillary findings were that users and librarians felt available time and information retrieval technologies had a major impact on the reference interaction. These suggest two additional areas for future research. Studies that investigate the time variable might focus more precisely on users' perceptions of the interaction at various points in the semester, when they were pressed for time and when they were less stressed. This type of study would add to the understanding of the dynamics of the interaction in times of stress and help identify coping techniques for users and librarians.

Studies that investigate information retrieval technologies might delve more deeply into their effect on relational factors in the interaction. For example, librarians discussed encountering users with "computer phobia." How does this affect perceptions of success in the encounter? How can librarians and users minimize negative affect (i.e., feelings)? How does the librarian's attitude toward "phobic" users help or hinder the interaction's success? Use of information retrieval technologies is receiving increasing attention in the library/information science literature, but no studies have looked at interpersonal impacts.

The barrier of lack of self-disclosure is another possibility for future investigation. There is a large body of literature on self-disclosure[14] and deception[15] that could be used to develop an understanding and perhaps ways of coping with surrogate users.

This study found that users reported more perceptions of the librarians' nonverbal behavior than librarians reported of users' nonverbal behavior. This finding suggests that investigations of nonverbal approachability could provide valuable insights for librarians seeking to understand nonverbal behavior as both facilitator and barrier. For example, Marie L. Radford has studied nonverbal approachability and identified positive and negative non-verbal behaviors that can invite the approach of users or repel them.[16] To date, however, there have been very few scientific studies of nonverbal behavior in the librarian–user interaction.

Qualitative methods, such as interviewing, the critical incident technique, and the paired perception analysis, are increasingly being applied in library research.[17] Qualitative research methods were effective here in exploring and forming understanding of the librarian–user interaction. The dynamic and multifaceted nature of this interaction requires a method of study that recognizes its complexity. Also, context is vitally important in investigations of human interaction. Qualitative methodology seeks to preserve the context surrounding the phenomenon it investigates. Continued application of qualitative methods is highly recommended in future research of librarian–user interaction.

Limitations

Although the qualitative methods in the present study proved very effective, they also had several limitations. These results are considered exploratory in nature. They are exploratory because the sample studied is small. As noted in chapter 4, a small sample size is common in qualitative research.[18] This sample size was chosen to allow for a thorough analysis of the large amount of interview data that was generated. Also, because of the constraints imposed by the field setting, librarian and user participants could not be randomly selected. Therefore, these findings cannot be generalized to larger populations without further study. In addition, because the research was conducted at three academic sites, no generalization can be claimed to other types of libraries such as special, school, or public libraries.

Data-gathering techniques used in this study depended, for the most part, on user and librarian self-report. There was nonparticipant observation of the interactions that served to contextualize the data, not to make independent judgments of issues such as the success or accuracy of the information. The basis of the analysis is, therefore, the subjective perceptions of the participants. In addition, the analytical procedures were largely based on the subjective decisions of the researcher in developing the category and coding schemes. As a check on this, samples of the data from the critical incident and paired perception analysis were sent to two additional pairs of raters as a reliability check.[19]

Analysis was also limited by the use of audio- rather than videotapes. Use of audiotapes focused analysis on verbal expressions and precluded use of nonverbal data that would be available from visual cues. In addition, the audiotapes were transcribed and analysis concentrated primarily on the interview transcripts. Nonverbal behaviors such as laughs and pauses were noted, but analysis focused primarily on the verbal data. As noted in the findings and discussion chapters, nonverbal behaviors play an important role in the interpersonal communication process. Users, especially, revealed sensitivity to their perceptions of the librarian's nonverbal cues. It is recommended that future studies strive to include both verbal and nonverbal components, perhaps utilizing videotaping and coding of nonverbal behaviors.

Another limitation concerns the possibility of the Hawthorne effect.[20] This suggests that people may change their behavior when they know they are being observed. In this study, both users and librarians may have been affected by the data collection process that was obtrusive, in that librarians and users were interrupted in their work to be interviewed. Reports of perceptions of success by users may have been influenced by the knowledge that their responses were being tape-recorded, although they were reassured of the confidentiality of this record. One user was observed to have hesitated when recalling a negative critical incident and to glance around the office in which the interview was being conducted to make sure the librarian was not around. The user then related a critical incident that had taken place in a different library, thus deciding that he or she could not chance being overheard, although the librarian in question was not present in the building.

Librarians may have been even more susceptible to the Hawthorne effect. Unlike users, they knew that they were being observed and that questions would be asked of the users and themselves regarding specific interactions. Librarians may have reacted to this by being unusually friendly, patient, or thorough. Interestingly, some evidence was offered that suggests that librarians did *not* change their behavior in ways that were noticeable to the users. During postinteraction interviews, three of the twenty-nine users (10%) revealed that they had previously interacted with the same librarians. All three reported that they had noticed *no difference* between the librarian's previous behavior and the present interaction. When asked about this, one user's response was:

> User: I think she was very nice and helpful and pleasant.
> Interviewer: So you would say today she was not affected by my watching?
> User: No, I don't think so. (U08)

Another user at first said there was no difference but, when pressed, admitted that:

> User: I guess maybe a little bit more of attention, but not so much that I, I mean now that you bring it out, I kinda could say maybe there was a little bit more attention, but at the time I wasn't even ... but not overly wasn't like ...
> Interviewer: It wasn't noticeable to you until ...
> User: Yeah, until you just said it now ... yeah, exactly, 'cause I remember last time she was just as helpful and I don't think she was being interviewed by another graduate student.(U26)

This is of interest, because usually in field work of this nature, there is no previous encounter to compare with the interaction being studied. This is also notable because it suggests that more often than has been assumed librarian–user interactions may a *sequence* of encounters rather than just isolated events.

Pragmatic Implications/Recommendations

This research has several important practical implications for:
- graduate education of librarians;
- continuing education, reeducation, and in-service education;
- recruitment of librarians and graduate students;
- working with increasingly diverse library populations;
- development and implementation of reference and other service policy statements;
- evaluation of reference librarians;
- instruction of library users.

These implications are discussed in detail below.

At the present time, librarian education is centered on reference sources and systems. For the most part, it treats interpersonal communication processes superficially. This study found that the relational dimensions of communication are critical to user assessment of the quality of reference service. These findings support the views of others. Library schools need to recognize the importance of understanding the interpersonal communication process and the value of communication skills.[21] Robert S. Taylor noted that library schools have traditionally focused on the reference sources rather than on the "dynamics of communication."[22] Thompson R. Cummins points out that:

> The complexities of the interactions involved in this whole process are ones for which librarians are not in general trained. Most library schools ignore the interpersonal aspects of the reference encounter almost entirely.[23]

Sandra M. Black believes that until library schools recognize that interpersonal skills:

> are at least as important as cataloguing, and reflect this in their admissions procedures and their course approach, the personality of librarians and their ability to communicate effectively will not change.[24]

It would be extremely beneficial for librarians to increase their study of interpersonal dynamics in basic and advanced reference courses. The author recommends an entire course on interpersonal communication for all students of library science, with inclusion of additional study of communication processes as appropriate throughout core curricula and advanced courses.[25] Further, because users are sensitive to the librarian's attitude toward them, librarians need to be made aware of the importance of their verbal and nonverbal communication. Although many practitioners believe that "people skills" are inherent, research has shown that librarians can be educated to improve their interpersonal communication skills.[26]

Because most librarians currently in the field have not had formal education in communication, this research also points out the need for veteran librarians to attend continuing education courses or in-service workshops on communication. Even those who feel that they have good people skills can benefit greatly from refreshers and from being appraised of recently developed techniques or research findings.

The present study suggests that library schools should seek students with good interpersonal skills and outgoing personalities or, for those who are more reserved, with a high degree of sensitivity to others.[27] It also points out the need for replacement of the stereotypical images of the reference librarian, isolated and surrounded by dusty books in glass cases.[28] More current and accurate images may be ones in which the reference librarian is helping people to use books and information systems.

Comments from librarians interviewed reflect increasing enrollments of foreign and minority students.[29] To respond to this trend, libraries need to recruit minority and bilingual reference librarians. Second-language study should also be encouraged for prospective and practicing librarians. Every library should offer a list of speakers of foreign languages who would be willing to act as translators/interpreters in the reference process. This study reveals that it can be difficult for users and librarians to come to an understanding when they are both native speakers of the same language.[30] A language and/or cultural barrier makes clear communication even more difficult and frustrating. Mengxiong Liu and Bernice Redfern note that:

> Cultural diversity is a reality today. If librarians do not make an effort to study their more ethnically diverse patrons, misperceptions about these groups and their information needs will remain.[31]

This research also has implications for the development and implementation of reference and other service policy statements. A policy that defines success in reference interactions solely in terms of the accuracy of information delivery is inadequate. Reference policies (as well as other policies affecting service to users) need to include sections that define the desired interpersonal qualities in library service. The "Guidelines for Behavioral Performance of Reference and Information Professionals" provides an excellent template for establishing such policies.[32]

Other policy implications follow from the findings of this research. For example, the way the reference librarian's time is structured is exceedingly important. Because users perceive librarians' time limitations to be critical to success, it is vital, especially during busy periods, to have two or more librarians available. If additional help is not available, busy librarians can increase positive user perceptions by verbally or nonverbally signaling to waiting users that they will be helped as soon as possible.[33]

Also, distractions such as phones at the reference desk and responsibilities for hardware maintenance (e.g., changing paper or cartridges in printers) should be kept to an absolute minimum. If possible, student assistants or paraprofessionals should screen calls and attend to hardware "housekeeping" duties. Not only would this policy free librarians for longer interactions with users, but it would also increase their appearance of availability to users and decrease their personal stress levels that are communicated to users and colleagues.[34]

This study also has implications for evaluation of librarians. Its communication-centered findings call for an evaluation of librarians that gives *equal emphasis* to interpersonal aspects and accuracy. Often librarians are evaluated solely in terms of their accuracy and efficiency in answering reference questions, but this study found that establishing positive interpersonal relationships with each user is just as important. Librarians who are aware that relational aspects will be an important part of their performance evaluations would pay more attention to the information "given off" as well as to that "given."[35]

This study also has major implications for instruction of academic library users. Like librarian education, present bibliographic instruction and courses in library literacy focus attention on orienting users to locations of materials and familiarity with the use of information sources and systems. But this study shows it is extremely important for users to learn about the interpersonal dynamics of the interaction. It is recommended that basic library orientation focus increased attention on interpersonal aspects of library use. Users could certainly benefit from increased understanding of what librarians expect and value in the reference interaction. Users could also benefit from being made aware of the importance of planning for their research, allowing sufficient time, and being persistent (e.g., waiting during a busy time or returning for additional help when the librarian is available).

Users also would profit from an understanding of the importance of their attitude toward task and toward the librarian in the interaction. Users who are indifferent to the assignment may provoke a negative attitude in the librarians and form a barrier to achieving their goal.

Finally, more users should think of the librarian as ally rather than adversary in the reference process.

Value of the Study to Social Science Research and Theory

This study has provided results that may be useful to researchers, educators, and library practitioners who are interested in the librarian–user interaction. In addition, it may be of value to practitioners in other fields (such as doctors or lawyers) in which similar interactions take place.[36] Librarians, much like physicians, come to the interaction:

> as knowledgeable professionals "at home" in the environment in which the interactions are occurring . . . . They are familiar with terminology and protocols, able to routinely take medical histories and perform necessary physical exams and diagnostic procedures, and generally have substantial experience with the range of medical problems and circumstances which present themselves.[37]

The librarian "operates" from a comfortable, familiar environment—the reference desk—surrounded by the well-known reference materials and systems. Answering queries from users becomes a routine matter, indeed in the academic setting, the same library assignments are given to classes of students regularly each semester. With experience, these questions become easily "diagnosed" and tried-and-true reference sources "prescribed."[38] On the other hand, the user, like the patient, comes to the interaction:

looking for help . . . . They do so in an environment that is unfamiliar—one which they often perceive as intimidating . . . . Frequently they enter the interaction anxious about their health, and lacking medical knowledge or relevant professional expertise.[39]

Users, like patients, lack the technological knowledge and experience of the information provider—the librarian. This study has shown that the user also may be similarly intimidated or anxious about approaching and interacting with the librarian, and can be subject to severe time constraints. At busy parts of the semester, users may have to wait in a line at the reference desk, perhaps increasing their stress.

Considering these similarities, the findings from this research have potential application in other contexts in which a technically skilled or highly educated professional interacts with a client who is less knowledgeable. Future research might explore these relationships.

This study's application of qualitative research methods in the library context may encourage future research using similar techniques. The study illustrates three methods—development of a category scheme, critical incident technique, and analysis of paired perceptions—that may provide models for other research. In addition, vital interpersonal dimensions that this study identifies could be used as variables by future researchers.

Conclusion

This study has extended knowledge of the librarian–user interaction in two significant ways.

1. The study's three interlocking analyses have shown the importance of interpersonal aspects of the reference interaction.

2. The study has identified relational dimensions that are central to perceptions of success and failure.

The research reported in this book just begins to explore the dynamics of this complex interaction. Nevertheless, it does define many areas for future research. With increased understanding of this process, greater success and satisfaction for both users and librarians is possible, even in an era when sources, systems, and society are becoming ever more sophisticated.

Notes

1. Brenda Dervin, "Useful Theory for Librarianship: Communication, Not Information," *Drexel Library Quarterly* 13 (July 1977): 16–32.

2. Claude E. Shannon and Warren Weaver, *The Mathematical Theory of Communication.* (Urbana, Ill.: Univ. of Ill. Pr., 1949).

3. Brent D. Ruben. *Communication and Human Behavior.* 2nd ed. (New York: Macmillan, 1988).

4. John V. Richardson Jr., "Teaching General Reference Work: The Complete Paradigm and Competing Schools of Thought, 1890–1990," *Library Quarterly* 62 (Jan. 1992): 85.

5. Ibid., 85.

6. See Erving Goffman, *The Presentation of Self in Everyday Life* (Garden City, N.Y.: Doubleday Anchor, 1959); ———, *Behavior in Public Places: Notes on the Social Organization of Gatherings* (New York: The Free Pr., 1963; ———, *Interaction Ritual: Essays on Face-to-Face Behavior* (Garden City, N.Y.: Anchor, 1967); ———, *Relations in Public: Microstudies of the Public Order* (New York: Basic Bks., 1971); and ———, *Forms of Talk* (Philadelphia: Univ. of Pennsylvania Pr., 1981); see also Kenneth Burke, *A Grammar of Motives* (New York: Prentice Hall, 1952); C. Wright Mills, "Situated Actions and Vocabularies of Motive," *American Sociological Review* 5 (Dec. 1940): 904–13.

7. James T. Tedeschi. *Impression Management: Theory and Social Psychological Research* (New York: Academic Pr., 1981), 3.

8. See Tedeschi, *Impression Management,* for an overview of these projects.

9. Mary Kathleen Chelton, "Adult–Adolescent Service Encounters: The Library Context," (Ph.D. diss., Rutgers—State Univ. of New Jersey, 1997).

10. For an excellent description of social exchange theory, see Michael E. Roloff, *Interpersonal Communication: The Social Exchange Approach* (Beverly Hills, Calif.: Sage, 1981); see also Harold H. Kelley and John W. Thibaut, *Interpersonal Relations; A Theory of Interdependence* (New York: John Wiley, 1978).

11. Stephen J. Littlejohn, *Theories of Human Communication,* 5th ed. (Belmont, Calif.: Wadsworth, 1996), 264.

12. See, for example, Ellen Berscheid, "Interpersonal Attraction," in *Handbook of Social Psychology* Vol. 2., 3rd ed., ed. G. Lindzey & E. Aronson. (New York: Random House, 1985), 413–84; Ellen Berscheid and Elaine Hatfield, *Interpersonal Attraction,* 2nd ed. (Reading, Mass.: Addison-Wesley, 1978).

13. See Michael E. Roloff, *Interpersonal Communication: The Social Exchange Approach* (Beverly Hills, Calif.: Sage, 1981).

14. See, for example, Mark J. Thompson, Nathan M. Smith, and Bonnie L. Woods, "A Proposed Model of Self-Disclosure," *RQ* 20 (winter 1980): 160–64.

15. See D. G. Ellis, "Interpersonal Deception: Theory and Critique," *Communication Theory* 6 (1996): Special issue; M. Zucherman and R. E. Driver, "Telling Lies: Verbal and Nonverbal Correlates of Deception," in *Multi-channel Integrations of Nonverbal Behavior,* ed. Aron W. Siegman and Stanley Feldstein (Hillsdale, N.J.: Erlbaum, 1985), 129–48.

16. Marie L. Radford, "A Qualitative Investigation of Nonverbal Immediacy in the User's Decision to Approach the Academic Reference Librarian," presented at the Library Research Seminar I, Florida State Univ., Tallahassee, Fla., Nov. 1–2, 1996.

17. See Constance A. Mellon, *Naturalistic Inquiry for Library Science: Methods and Applications for Research, Evaluation, and Teaching* (New York: Greenwood, 1990).

18. Jana Bradley, "Methodological Issues and Practices in Qualitative Research," *Library Quarterly* 63 (Oct. 1993): 431–49.

19. See Marie L. Radford, "Relational Aspects of Reference Interactions: A Qualitative Investigation of the Perceptions of Users and Librarians in the Academic Library" (Ph.D. diss., Rutgers—State Univ. of New Jersey, 1993), 157–59, 180–81, for a detailed description of the reliability checks.

20. F. J. Roethlisberger and William J. Dickson, *Management and the Worker*, (Cambridge, Mass.: Harvard Univ. Pr., 1939).

21. See, for example, Patricia Dewdney, "The Effects of Training Reference Librarians in Interview Skills: A Field Experiment," (Ph.D. diss., School of Library and Information Service, Univ. of Western Ontario, 1986); Helen M. Gothberg, *Training Library Communication Skills: Development of 3 Video Tape Workshops* (Tuscon, Ariz.: Univ. of Ariz., 1977). ERIC Document 163 934; Barron Holland, "Updating Library Reference Services through Training for Interpersonal Competence," *RQ* 17 (spring 1978): 207–11; Benita J. Howell, Edward B. Reeves, and John van Willigen, "Fleeting Encounters—A Role Analysis of Reference Librarian-Patron Interaction," *RQ* 16 (winter 1976): 124–29; Patrick R. Penland, *Communication for Librarians* (Pittsburgh: Univ. of Pittsburgh, 1971); Sally Stevenson, *Performance Appraisal for Librarians: A Guided Self-Study Approach* (Albany, N.Y.: State Univ. of N.Y., 1980). ERIC Document 234 804.

22. Robert S. Taylor, "Question Negotiation and Information Seeking in Libraries," *College & Research Libraries* 29 (May 1968): 191.

23. Thompson R. Cummins, "Question Clarification in the Reference Encounter," *Canadian Library Journal* 41 (Apr. 1984), 66.

24. Sandra M. Black, "Personality—Librarians as Communicators," *Canadian Library Journal* 38 (Apr. 1981): 71.

25. The author has developed and taught a course of this nature titled "Interpersonal Communication for Information Professionals" at Pratt Institute, Brooklyn, N.Y. Student feedback indicates that they find the course to be extremely valuable to their professional development. A syllabus is available from the author upon request.

26. Patricia Dewdney, "The Effects of Training Reference Librarians in Interview Skills: A Field Experiment" (Ph.D. diss., School of Library and Information Service, Univ. of Western Ontario, 1986).

27. See also Black, "Personality."

28. See Gary P. Radford, "Positivism, Foucault, and the Fantasia of the Library: Conceptions of Knowledge and the Modern Library Experience," *Library Quarterly* 62 (Oct. 1992): 408–24; and Marie L. Radford and Gary P. Radford, "Power, Knowledge, and Fear: Feminism, Foucault and the Stereotype of the Female Li-

brarian," *Library Quarterly* 67 (July 1997): 250–66.

29. See Mary Beth Allen, "International Students in Academic Libraries: A User Survey," *College & Research Libraries* 54 (July 1993): 323–33; Mengxiong Liu and Bernice Redfern, "Information-Seeking Behavior of Multicultural Students: A Case Study at San Jose State Univ.," *College & Research Libraries* 58 (July 1997): 348–54; Ziming Liu, "Difficulties and Characteristics of Students from Developing Countries in Using American Libraries," *College & Research Libraries* 54 (Jan. 1993): 25–31; Irene Hoffmann and Opritsa Popa, "Library Orientation and Instruction for International Students: The Univ. of Calif.-Davis Experience," *RQ* 25 (spring 1986): 356–60; R. Errol Lam, "The Reference Interview: Some Intercultural Considerations," *RQ* 27 (spring 1988): 390–95; Veronica Nance-Mitchell, "A Multicultural Library: Strategies for the Twenty-First Century," *College & Research Libraries* 57 (Sept., 1996): 405–13; Kwasi Sarkodie-Mensah, "Dealing with International Students in a Multicultural Era," *Journal of Academic Librarianship* 18 (Sept. 1992): 214–16.

30. See also Patricia Dewdney and Catherine Sheldrick Ross, "Flying a Light Aircraft: Reference Service Evaluation from the User's Viewpoint," *RQ* 34 (winter 1994): 217–30.

31. Liu and Redfern, "Information-Seeking Behavior of Multicultural Students," 353.

32. "Guidelines for Behavioral Performance of Reference and Information Services Professionals," *RQ* 36 (winter 1996): 200–3.

33. See Helen Gothberg, "Immediacy: A Study of Communication Effect of the Reference Process," *Journal of Academic Librarianship* 2 (July 1976): 126–29; Radford, "A Qualitative Investigation of Nonverbal Immediacy."

34. See K. D. Hickey, "Technostress in Libraries and Media Centers: Case Studies and Coping Strategies," *TechTrends* 37, (1992): 17–20; John Kupersmith, "Technostress and the Reference Librarian," *Reference Services Review* 20 (spring, 1992): 7–14+.

35. See also Goffman, *The Presentation of Self in Everyday Life*, and Kenneth Pease, *Communication with and without Words* (Warwickshire: Vernon Scott Associates, 1974).

36. See Dervin, "Useful Theory for Librarianship"; Thomas Lee Eichman, "The Complex Nature of Opening Reference Questions," *RQ* 17 (1978): 212–22; Rachael Naismith, "Reference Communication: Commonalities in the Worlds of Medicine and Librarianship," *College & Research Libraries* 57 (Jan. 1996): 44–57; Carolyn J. Radcliff, "Interpersonal Communication with Library Patrons: Physician–Patient Research Models," *RQ* 34 (summer 1995): 497–506; Marilyn Domas White, "Evaluation of the Reference Interview," *RQ* 25 (fall 1985): 76–85.

37. Brent D. Ruben, "The Health Caregiver–Patient Relationship: Pathology, Etiology, Treatment," in *Communication and Health: Systems Perspective*, ed. Eileen B. Ray and Lewis Donohew (Hillsdale, N.J.: L. Erlbaum Associates, 1990), 52.

38. White, "Evaluation of the Reference Interview."

39. Ruben, "The Health Caregiver–Patient Relationship," 52.

Appendix A

Data Collection Forms

❦ ❦ ❦ ❦ ❦ ❦ ❦ ❦ ❦

Data Collection Form—User Profile

U- _____

1. Date of interview: _____   _____

2. Place of interview:_____

3. Sex: _____

4. Level: (circle one)
   freshman   sophomore   junior   senior
   graduate   faculty   other_____

5. Name of institution you attend (or faculty where you teach):_____

6. Major field of study:_____

7. Type of institution (circle one):
   community college   primarily undergraduate college
   research university   other (describe)_____

8. Thinking back over the past two semesters, how often did you go to the library (circle the one that most closely resembles your use)?
   never   every day   other (describe)_____
   less than once/semester   1–3x/semester   4–6x/semester
   more than 6x/semester

9. For what purposes do you use the library? Please circle.
    a. studying   d. return books   g. use AV or computers
    b. research   e. library instruction   h. meet friends
    c. borrow books   f. class in library   i. other (describe):

    _____

10. Thinking back over the past two semesters, how often did you ask a
     reference librarian for information or help?
     never   every day   other (describe)_____
     less than once/semester   1–3x/semester   4–6x/semester
     more than 6x/semester

11. Age: _____

Data Collection Form—Librarian Profile

L-_____

1. Date of interview: _____   _____

2. Time of interview: _____

3. Place of interview: _____
    _____

4. Sex: _____

5. Degrees held, major field of study, and institution awarding:
    B.A. _____ year_____
    MLS _____ year_____
    other_____ year_____
    other_____ year_____

6. Present position: _____
    _____

7. Name of institution of present position:
    _____
    _____

8. Hours per week in present position in interaction with users:
at reference desk _____ other (describe)_____

9. Type of institution of present position (circle one):
community college   primarily undergraduate college
research university   other (describe)_____

10. Number of years experience in academic reference: _____

11. Number of years experience in reference other than academic (please describe): _____
_____

12. Age:_____

Appendix B

Informed Consent and Information Sheet

❧❧ ❧❧ ❧❧ ❧❧ ❧❧ ❧❧ ❧❧ ❧❧ ❧❧

My name is Marie Radford. I am a doctoral student at Rutgers University currently working on my dissertation. In order to gather the necessary information for my research, I am conducting many individual interviews of librarians and library users. I deeply appreciate your willingness to participate in this project.

Before we start this interview, I would like to reassure you that as a participant in this project you have several very definite rights.
- First, your participation in this interview is entirely voluntary.
- You are free to refuse to answer any question at any time.
- You are free to withdraw from the interview at any time.
- This interview will be kept strictly confidential and will be used only for scholarly research.
- Excerpts of this interview may be made part of a final research dissertation. Under no circumstances will your name or identifying characteristics be included in this dissertation.

I would be grateful if you would sign this form to show that I have read you its contents.

_____ (signed)

_____ (printed)

_____ (dated)

If you have any further questions, you may contact me at (201) 595-3193. Thank you.

(Form adapted from Lofland & Lofland, 1984, and Dr. H. Mokros)

Appendix C

Main Study Interview Questions

❧ ❧ ❧ ❧ ❧ ❧ ❧ ❧ ❧

Preinteraction Questions for Librarians

1. What, for you, is the purpose of the reference interview?

2. Thinking back, can you recall a reference interview that you would consider particularly successful. Describe it. What, for you, made it successful?

3. Again, thinking back, can you recall a reference interview that you would consider particularly unsuccessful? Describe it. What, for you, made it unsuccessful?

4. How do you vary your technique among users?

5. In your mind, in reference interviews, what kind of qualities does a good library user have?

6. In your mind, in reference interviews, what kind of qualities does a poor user have? Have you known one? If yes, what were the things you remember best about him or her?

7. What would you say would be the qualities that a good reference librarian would have? Could you put these in order by importance?

8. What would you say would be the qualities that a poor reference librarian would have?

9. When you consider the important qualities of interactions, do you feel that new information technologies have an impact upon your work? If so, how?

Postinteraction Questions for Librarians

1. Would you please describe what happened?

2. How do you think it went?

3. Looking back on the interaction, what was important to you?

4. Do you think the user got the help he or she wanted? Why or why not?

5. How did the interaction measure up? Would you have changed anything if you could go back and do it again?

Postinteraction Questions for Users

1. A few minutes ago, you spoke to the reference librarian. Would you please describe what happened?

2. How do you think it went?

3. Did you get the help you needed? Why or why not?

4. If you needed help again, would you go back to the same person? Why or why not?

5. How useful was this discussion with the reference librarian to you? Why?

6. What, for you, are your goals or aims when you ask a librarian for help?

7. Thinking back over past times when you asked a librarian for help, can you recall a situation in which you were very pleased? Describe it.

8. Why were you pleased?

9. Again, thinking back over past times when you asked a librarian for help, can you recall a situation in which you were displeased? Describe it.

10. Why were you displeased?

11. How would you have changed this discussion if you could?

Appendix D

Observation Forms

❦ ❦ ❦ ❦ ❦ ❦ ❦ ❦ ❦

Observation Form A

Site_____
Librarian # _____
Date_____ Time _____ to _____

Activities noted during this time:
_____number of users
_____phone calls
_____computer problems _____
_____queue of users _____
_____missing reference materials_____
_____unusual circumstances _____
_____security problem_____
_____other librarian present _____
_____work left to be done_____
_____repair/maintenance work being done_____

Comments on activity level:_____
_____
_____
_____
_____

General notes: _____
_____
_____
_____
_____
_____
_____

Observation Form B

Site_____

User #_____ Sex _____

Date_____

Time _____ to _____ Duration _____

Topic or query _____
_____
_____

Notes:
_____
_____
_____
_____
_____
_____
_____
_____
_____
_____
_____
_____
_____

Appendix E

Sample Librarian and User Interview Transcripts

❦❧ ❦❧ ❦❧ ❦❧ ❦❧ ❦❧ ❦❧ ❦❧ ❦❧

A. Sample Librarian Preinteraction Interview
Interview with L-04
I. Let's just start off with kind of a textbook question. What, for you, is the *purpose* of the reference interview?

L-04. To understand what the question is exactly, not the initial question that you get, but what the patron is *really* after and you're also trying to do two other things at the same time, understand the general background of the patron so that the question can be placed in perspective and with that understanding you can recommend further . . . research that the patron may not have thought of as, um, possible . . . expansion areas for the research. So you're, first of all, you're trying to establish the, ah, . . . the level at which you're expected to work with him or her and then the general context of the question, is it for a course, what is the course, and so on, and what is the major of the student, that type of background, general background information, and then how can I suggest things that may not have even occurred to him or her that would further inform the process.

I. Okay. If you could think back and recall a reference interview, either it could have been today or some other occasion, that you considered particularly successful

L-04. Hummm.

I. . . . and describe it for me.

L-04. Well, let's see . . . . hummm . . . . Well, one thing that comes to mind is . . . I can't think of anything specific, but I've had many . . . many instances where the patron comes and says this is what I'm looking for

I. Um hum.

L-04. . . . and by the time we're done with the reference interview, the goal is clarified and it's *substantially* different from the initial question. In other words, one of the things I've noticed consistently, or one thing that happens quite often, is that the patron comes with a vague question.

I. Um hum

L-04. Sometimes the patron has difficulty . . . formulating the question, so part of the reference librarian's responsibility is to clarify the *real* research goal with the patron. So you ask probing questions. I think it *really* helps if you also know the subject[1] . . .

I. Um hum.

L-04. . . . area. I think I perform much better, for example, in the case of questions in the field of education.

I. Um hum.

L-04. There are a lot of students here doing master's theses in education. If they if they come to me with research questions on that, I think I'm *far* more effective than, let's say, if it's a law . . .

I. Um hum.

L-04. . . . question of law.

I. Um hum. Could you recall any specific time?

L-04. Specifics something. No, I just can't remember something right now that . . .

I. Well, maybe it will come to you as we're talking . . .

L-04. Okay.

I. . . . about other things. My next question might be a little bit easier, I hope. If you can think back and recall a reference interaction which you would consider particularly *unsuccessful* . . .

L-04. Unsuccessful . . .

I. . . . and describe it for me . . . . I find that most librarians kind of have their story about {laugh from L} either a problem patron . . .

L-04. That's terrible.

I. . . . or something that happened that they remember.

L-04. Hum. Again, I can't think of anything specific but I remember patterns, which is this is actually true of the way I think and remember. I'm not very good when it comes to remembering particulars, but what I'm very good [at is] in remembering patterns . . .

I. Okay.

L-04. . . . and this is just a natural product of, I think, my training in philosophy. What I'm looking for [is] the overall truth rather than specifics. So the pattern of bad things that happen that I remember is a patron that comes to you with very strong preconceptions of what a librarian is, and they're usually bad ideas about who a librarian is and a, you can sense this in how abrupt they are, and they're almost *expecting* you not to care or *expecting* you not to be responsive or *expecting* you to be unprofessional or even dumb, so they're kind of impatient . . .

I. Um hum.

L-04. . . . with you because even though they're asking you the question, they expect to be frustrated so those are the *most* difficult, ah, patrons. I have to spend the first part of the reference interview in a way demonstrating to them that they're dealing with some one else, you know. I try to somehow catch their attention or impress them *somehow* so that they will be shocked into to saying, Wait a minute, this is not, this is not the, this is going to be different."

I. Why do you think they have those preconceived . . .

L-04. Well . . .

I. . . . preconceived ideas?

L-04. Sadly, in many cases it is because a lot of librarians are ill prepared *and are* unprofessional.

I. Um hum.

L-04. I mean I am not. There are good reasons why they have this impression but . . . it is also true that the field has been growing and changing in the past decade or two so that . . . I am very hopeful that in the 21st century with the advent of information technology, the status and prestige of the profession will rise and people will really see information professionals with a different

I. Um hum.

L-04. . . . it's happening already.

I. Um hum.

L-04. I'm already seeing this. I'm *clearly* seeing it in the corporate world, corporate libraries. I'm also seeing it in good academic libraries, but it, ah, you know, these types of stereotypes change very very slowly.

I. Okay. I was just curious to ask that even though it wasn't one of my . . .

L-04. Okay.

I. . . . prepared questions. Do you vary your, you were talking before about different levels of users in your in your... goal of the reference interview, you were saying that one of the things you have to do is determine the level. Do you vary your technique among users? Could you talk about that a little bit?

L-04. Oh yes, depending on what my perceived level is.

I. Yes, yes.

L-04. *Oh*, naturally, I mean especially, let's say in the state libraries or public libraries when anyone can walk in. In academic libraries, it's a more select group, essentially faculty member and graduate students, or college students

I. Um hum.

L-04. But in public libraries in [site C] anyone can walk in and use it. The first thing you have to determine is are they high school students, freshman, sophomores, or upper classmen, junior seniors, that makes a difference. What's their major? What is this particular course? Is it the term paper, one term paper for the entire semester? Or just a short three-page paper. Those are the kinds of things that are going to give me an idea about level. I'm also always paying attention to how bright they are.

I. Um hum.

L-04. I have an assessment of how intelligent this person is, how much can I challenge him? How motivated is he or she? I try to, sometimes by asking direct questions, figure out how much time do they intend to spend on this . . . you know . . . I try to get a sense of how much time do they plan to stay in the library *today* you know, and then you know based on that, well, I say, well, maybe we can do part of the work now and we can do this first. We can then go do some reading and then come back and follow up with someone else or with me if I'm here next, two sundays from now. *That* kind of thing so that level understood in the broadest sense, I mean level and the general context of the reference question.

I. Um hum, and so you make that assessment by actually asking questions.

L-04. I ask them, oh yes, I ask them questions. A lot of times, they're not gonna know enough to give that information to you. In other words they're not professionals after all.

I. Right.

L-04. They're *lay* people, if you will, when it comes to information, so it is your job actually to ferret out those issues that *you know* are important for the reference interview.

I. Um hum.

L-04. That's your job.

I. Okay. Now I'm going to ask you in your mind, in reference interviews what kind of qualities does a good library *user* have. We'll talk about the user *first*.

L-04. Hummm . . . I guess number one would have to be their genuine desire to find the answer to the question, their level of motivation and interest... that's certainly the best desirable quality.

I. Genuine as opposed to?

L-04. As opposed to because the teacher wants me to do it. You know, it's an assignment. I just want to get it over with or, you know, . . .

I. . . . the easiest way.

L-04. . . . something like that. Yeah, what's the easiest way of getting this done and going out and playing hookey or something. You see, then that's kind of . . .

I. Un huh.

L-04. . . . demoralizing to me, . . .

I. Yeah.

L-04. . . . you know.

I. Are there other qualities? Other than that genuine desire?

L-04. Well, certainly I always enjoy working with someone who has broad knowledge.

I. Um hum.

L-04. Renaissance men and women are always fun to work with because then it becomes I learn from them, too, as we're doing the research together, you know. They tell me things that people who are *excited* about learning and knowing as an end in itself.

I. Um hum.

L-04. You can feel that very quickly and easily, and then, you know, I become like, we become, like a little team working on this thing together, a sense of solving the puzzle or discovering the answer, figuring it out . . .

I. Um hum.

L-04. That type of *fun*.

I. Um hum.

L-04. It becomes fun. I love those types. That's a very positive thing in a user, too. Another one is someone who communicates well. I mean, after all, that's a very distinct skill, not, that not many people have. Someone who has good language skills, good communication skills, so that when I ask something, they answer the question rather than missing the point or they are simply effective in defining their need . . .

I. Um hum.

L-04. . . . and assertive, not apologizing profusely and being timid and insecure about their knowledge threatened by the library. Those are weaknesses. You have to work with them because the majority of patrons, unfortunately, will be like that.

I. Um hum. Well, that's what I want to ask about next, so we're getting right into it. What kind of qualities, then, does a poor user have? You mentioned some of them were somewhat like that. Yeah, uh huh.

L-04. In a way, I ended up mentioning them inadvertently, so, yeah, the person who's not genuinely interested in doing the research, the motivation is from without . . .

I. Um hum.

L-04. . . . and a dull person, a dull intellect or just lack of knowledge about the world in general.

I. Okay, we don't have to . . .

L-04. In a way, it's like the reverse almost, isn't it? like . . .

I. Yeah, yeah, yeah.

L-04. Yeah.

I. You were kind of talking around and about it. Okay, let's talk about librarians then. What would you say would be the qualities that a good or even *ideal* reference librarian would have?

L-04. Okay, *the* thing that helps the most is broad liberal arts foundation. I mean, I have noticed this very clearly. The *good* librarians are the ones who are curious about everything. They have read widely, they have a good liberal arts education, the bachelor's is not in a very, you know, let's say engineering.

I. Um hum. Um hum.

L-04. . . . it's more liberal arts. That works better and then, *and then,* the ones that have gone on and gotten a subject master's and they are doing reference work *in that subject.*[2] That's a *very* good librarian, and then they have an MLS . . . MLS and a subject master's beyond that they are people who enjoy helping others. There is this in this sense it is similar to teaching. It's a calling. The good librarians are ones that are *genuinely* interested in working with people, helping them, you know, teaching them. There is a component of teaching involved, that feeling of being the teacher, the guide.

I. Um hum.

L-04. If you enjoy that, then you'll be a good librarian. People who have good people skills, who are able to communicate smoothly and understand others. Are they good listeners, they catch social clues easily, if they have a multicultural background,[3] it's a *major* plus because so often an American librarian will misunderstand, *really* misunderstand, a Japanese freshman.

I. Um hum.

L-04. *Really,* because the body language and so on, the values, they are *significantly* different. See, that helps a lot.

I. I think, just personally, think that's been really overlooked in training of librarians, the intercultural . . .

L-04. Yeah, cross-cultural.

I. . . . communication processes.

L-04. Yeah, that's very true.

I. It's not in the curriculum *yet*.

L-04. There is no course like that.

I. Maybe soon as we go, maybe we'll see. {laugh} I didn't want to interrupt you.

L-04. They have to make it into two years, the MLS [one year is just, it's impossible

I. Well, I don't know. {laugh}

L-04. There is no time to do that.

I. Yeah, yeah.

L-04. If you're really going to do that kind of thing the MLS *must* be two years.

I. Yeah. You mentioned really kind of three qualities, the broad, liberal arts type knowledge of, and a subject knowledge, the teacher kind of skills, and the people kind of skills. If you had to rank them as to or talk about the relationship of which one would be more important, could you do that?

L-04. Ummmm.

I. Could, do you think they are in the order that you mentioned them in? of importance?

L-04. Yeah, but they're very close, aren't they? I mean, if someone is a very well educated, but he's a misanthrope, it's just not going to do any good. It's very similar to the idea of these professors who are masters of their fields, very knowledgeable, but they are terrible teachers.

I. Um hum.

L-04. So one becomes useless without the other, so they're in that sense I must say it's equally important that the person have the knowledge and have the desire and the ability to then share it. Otherwise the knowledge is not gonna help . . .

I. Okay.

L-04. . . . the reference process.

I. Okay, very good. Okay, then I guess the flip side of that. What would be the qualities that a *poor* librarian would have? Poor reference librarian would have, so you already mentioned a misanthrope or a . . .

L-04. Yeah, some kind of a, some, there are quite a few librarians I have met who have gone into the field just to hide in the library.

I. Um hum.

L-04. You get the sense somehow that this person is somehow, loves books, you know, loves learning and so on and reading but is a shy, private person and chose this profession just so he could go in the library and hide in the corner and not do much, that type of thing. And maybe they tried to get into technical services, but they didn't really like it and then they ended up in the reference department just like the other choice, if you will, and . . . but they're not *really* interested in dealing with people. And sometimes they're eccentric and insecure because of this negative stereotype of the profession. They see themselves as kind of a subprofession so they don't have a high, good self esteem.

I. Um hum.

L-04. . . . and that personal security other professional has, you know, really, ah, providing a valuable service there.

I. That's interesting.

L-04. So those librarians who fall into that trap and start kind of deprecating themselves, and they were not really interested in librarianship as a science but they chose it as, "Well, this is something I can handle." In other words, they became librarians for the wrong reasons.

I. Um hum.

L-04. It's a one-year program, it's a profession, that type of thing, as one of professors at [site X] once said, "You know, it's clean, it's indoors, {shared laughter}, the pay is decent." You know *those* kinds of reasons. I think to really be a good librarian you have to go into the profession because you are fascinated by information technology and information science[4] and you believe in the value of this field . . .

I. Um hum.

L-04. . . . to the twenty-first century. I'm talking about the people who are going into it now. But even, you know, you could say the same thing for two generations, librarians of two generations ago. In other words, are you *really* interested, so the bad ones are the ones that . . . took it just as a profession . . .

I. Um hum.

L-04. . . . something, something to do and it shows, it shows. Other things, well, I've already mentioned them—communication skills, people skills— these are partly learned and some of it is just a gift,[5] you know, and some people are talented, you know. Even in children, you see some children who are more sensitive to others, better able to communicate and so on and so forth. Maybe it's just the upbringing, the family, and so on, the quality of their education, elementary and secondary school, and so on and so forth. So . . .

I. Okay. That's a pretty, ah, good picture. Just one more question, um, and we, again you started to talk about this a little bit, when you consider these important qualities of interaction that you've been talking about, do you personally feel that the new information technologies have had an impact on *your* work?

L-04. Yes.

I. And how?

L-04. Yes, they've certainly enhanced, ah, my ability to provide information more efficiently, and just the breadth and the depth of the information has increased.

I. Do you think that the interaction, when you're using the information technologies with a patron who's come with a question, do you think that the quality of the interaction is changed by those technologies?

L-04. Um, not particularly, not the reference interview per se. No they do seem to be rather independent. It's a tool.

I. Um hum.

L-04. What's happening, *really.* I guess the crux of what's happening is, instead of using the paper sources, . . .

I. Right.

L-04. . . . you're using the online or the CD-Rom sources . . .

I. Right.

L-04. . . . and so on and so forth. Now there are some minor areas where it is impacting some patrons have computer phobia . . .

I. Um hum.

L-04. . . . so the, sometimes if you always have been threatened by it, feeling intimidated by it, . . .

I. Right.

L-04. . . . so that does make a difference. But it's minor, minor factor because it's fairly easy to set them at ease, and if you feel that this is what's happening you just spend a little more time with them at the computer and so on.

I. Do you think that it does? I was going to ask about that, the variable of time. Do you think that you spend more time with them because of the new technologies, or less time . . .

L-04. Ummmmmm.

I. . . . or is it about the same?

L-04. It's more an issue of how much you're getting for your time, you know. The efficiency is really what you should, what sometimes what's happening is because of the, there is this access to *more* information. The patron who is genuinely interested gets really excited and starts digging in much more than he or she might have if it was paper sources, you know. There is this just the patron may only have an hour . . .

I. Right.

L-04. . . . you know, they *work*, a lot of these students here, they work full-time and are doing the master's part time . . .

I. Right.

L-04. . . . and so on. I mean it is *real*. They have children, they have families, and so on, so when they come it's not like they're a graduate student just engaged in the pursuit.

I. Yeah, unfortunately. {laugh}

L-04. Uunfortunately, this is the reality, two career families and so on. So what is happening is that you're still spending the hour, but you're getting a lot more out of it because the technology is giving it to you faster.

I. But you feel that the actual quality of the interaction hasn't really changed?

L-04. Fundamentally? No.

I. Okay, we'll stop this.

B. Sample User Postinteraction Interview
U07 about L07

I. A few minutes ago, you spoke to the reference librarian. Could you please just describe to me what happened?

U07. I was looking for, like, just a piece of literature that we could discuss in a writing class so she suggested, like, looking in the literature section here and so we looked up Hemingway just as, like, an example, and it listed books of Hemingway and then poems and we like narrowed it down to short stories. And they were, like, readings of Hemingway or whatever, and it's pretty nice here. They have, like, it prints out for ya. Like my school we have that but it, it's a little less a specific.

I. Uh huh, so could you take a book out of here if you found one that . . .

U07. I don't have a card. I lost my card at [another college], but I think that it, we could use them and [a different college] too.

I. Oh, that's good, that's good. So how do you think this interaction went?

U07. It was good. She was very helpful, it didn't bother her to spend extra time. I found what I needed.

I. Okay, actually, that was my next question. Did you get the help you needed?

U07. Yes.

I. Okay, if you needed help again, would you go back to the same person?

U07. Yes

I. And why?

U07. Just because, um, she took me right where I had to go and it wasn't, like, help yourself or whatever. She demonstrated how to work the machine.

I. Um hum. Okay, just talking in general for a minute about when you use a library. Could you tell me what are your goals or aims are when you ask a librarian for help?

U07. Just direction. There's a lot of times that I'm researching things and no idea where to find them in the library 'cause I have a communications paper coming up and it's on, like, verbal communication in an office and I'm definitely gonna ask for help.

I. In an office?

U07. Yeah.

I. Yeah.

U07. So, and there's not, like, specific authors I can think of or a subject even maybe like business so I'd say, like, I know in our library they're definitely overworked. Like, they're always running around trying to help people. [6] I don't know what else to say.

I. So you might come here, you mean? Because here there's . . .

U07. Yeah, well, it's, I think they're about the same.

I. Uh huh. They're overworked here too? {laugh}

U07. Yeah, exactly. Librarians, in general, there's, there's just so many students. So few.

I. Yeah. Do you think they're nice? Do you think that the librarians are nicer here or are they nicer where you are or about the same?

U07. About the same, I think.

I. So even though they're overworked, they still ...

U07. Yeah.

I. ... they give you ...

U07. Yeah, they're polite.

I. They're polite.

U07. Helpful.

I. And they give you, that's good. I want to ask you to think back over other times when you asked a librarian for help and recall a situation in which you were very pleased? Thought it really went well. Can you do that and describe it for me?

U07. I did an honor's project on judicial activism and something else, it was like the opposite, and I had to go through old cases, like Supreme Court cases, and the librarian went through them with me, directed me to, like, the law books and what would be helpful because it was a very, like, difficult subject to research and I found what I needed. They then, they had like other suggestions, like maybe a periodical or whatever.

I. Um hum. Could you just put your finger, 'cause you thought of that real quick, could you put your finger on exactly why you thought that was such a good interaction?

U07. 'Cause, like, *I* felt like I was in a lot of trouble because I knew little about this, so it was good that, like, they directed me {laugh} where I should go.

I. Right, right. Okay, good. And now, I want you to think back on past times and see if you can recall a time when you asked a librarian for help and you were displeased or it was not a good interaction and describe it for me?

U07. Um .... I'm trying to think ah ... most of the time it's been a good experience. Um, sometimes they have trouble with the computers. I don't know if they, I think they're getting better, but, ah, sometimes just even the mechanical part of it with the [changing the paper or something ...

I. Um hum. Have you ever had a time when a librarian um ... you not, you know, that you had trouble personally, using the stuff, but that you had trouble when you asked for help?

U07. No.

I. No, okay, that's *good* actually

U07. Yeah, yeah.

I. You're a lucky person. So that's the end of my questions. Let me turn this off.

Notes

1. Informant talks about subject (content) continually during this interview. It is a critical dimension for this person, librarian needs subject information, subject master's, in-depth knowledge, etc., very classic librarian viewpoint, mentions communication or "people skills" as do other librarians but never really gives up on subject as being primary.

2. Subject, subject, subject.

3. New point, I don't think anyone else has mentioned multicultural concerns, also this is a minority librarian, so from a multicultural background.

4. Classic content statement, go into the field because you are fascinated by information.

5. I get this from more than one librarian, that much of these skills are inherent and cannot be taught, you either have it or you don't. Although L says partly, the way he talks about it sounds like fully.

6. Interesting observation that librarians are overworked, always running around helping people.

Appendix F

Sample Critical Incidents

A. Sample User Positive Critical Incident
User Positive Incident - #7
User (U11) Relational—Positive Librarian Attitude toward User
I. Just exactly to find what you're looking for. I want you to think back over times in your life when you asked a librarian for help, maybe a long time ago, or in your high school career, or sometime in a public library, any setting, if you can remember a time when you asked a librarian for help and you were very pleased with what you got?

U11. Well, the instructor in the [college x] library was *very* helpful. He showed us how to use the computers, which was very helpful and he gave us the sense that if we needed any kind of help, just to go back to him.

I. Okay, if you could put your finger on it, what exactly, was it that made you feel that he was . . .

U11. His patience . . .

I. He was very patient?

U11. Yeah.

171

B. Sample User Negative Critical Incident
User Negative Incident - #3
User (U04) Content—Lack of Technical Knowledge

U04. Unpleasant. No. I've never met an unpleasant librarian, thank heavens. {laugh from I} Unsuccessful? Yeah, I can remember once when, I don't remember what it was about, I think it was biology maybe, and I needed to do a paper and she told me to use a computer and didn't tell me under what, didn't *know* under what, so even though I tried to use the computer, I didn't know where to start, didn't have anything specific to {something} couldn't understand it very well

I. Um hum. So what was it then, if you could put your finger on it, that made it unsuccessful?

U04. I guess it was [that] she didn't have any knowledge in the area, and I didn't have any knowledge in the area. I'm just learning about it, and that's what did it basically.

I. Um hum.

U04. If the librarian doesn't know about it, then she can't really help you with it.

I. But you didn't feel that she was unpleasant?

U04. Not at all, never had an unpleasant librarian.

I. So it was the, you enjoyed the interaction on one level. Was it pleasant on one level, but you didn't get the information that you wanted?

U04. That's right, yeah.

I. So for you that was unsuccessful.

U04. Um hum.

I. Okay, how, how would you have changed that discussion if you could have? That one that was unsuccessful?

U04. I guess I would have gone back and asked my teacher first for specifics and then asked her if she had any knowledge of the specifics.

I. Oh so you felt almost that it was something on your part.

U04. Maybe, yeah, maybe I could have done something more, not just expected the librarian to do that.

I. Yeah, yeah, sometimes if students aren't very clear about what it is they're looking for, it's hard for the librarian to help.

U04. We do expect a lot. We do expect a lot. Like the librarian's got to know it's not always like that.

C. Sample Librarian Positive Critical Incident
Librarian Positive Incident - #3
Librarian (L05) Content—Technical Knowledge. Minor themes: systems related/ retrieval of information/ accuracy, finding the "right answer"
L05. Then the student that I was just helping at the card catalog, she wanted books on whole-language approach

I. Um huh.

L05. And it's not a *subject* in the card catalog. So then I said, "Well, it must be language learning," and there was language acquisition and language arts and language study and teaching and things like that. So I showed her that and I said, you know, you just have to flip through the cards and look for ones that maybe mention whole language or that sound like they're teaching approaches . . . are things that you can use and then check the book, check the and so . . . contents or index and see if whole-language approach is in there. And then she *did* when she was looking through the drawer found a few cards with whole language in the title.

I. Um hum.

L05. So then she was happy about that and then I checked the title side and it was the . . .

I. {something unintelligible} Yeah, yeah.

L05. . . . title of a few books which] began with whole language so that was good for her.

I. What do you think, for you makes if you were to think about the thing, that makes you feel that an interaction is successful? What are the things that . . .

L05. I, what I like to do is to, besides answering the question, is to try to explain a little bit about how libraries are organized and how *information* is organized *in* the library. And how that then you find what they want . . .

I. Um hum.

L05. . . . and sometimes explain to them that it may not be in the form that they have in mind or they have to use certain tools or different approaches that they didn't realize so . . . that's, like, you know, and try to help them see where they're how they can find what they want in the library . . .

I. Um hum.

L05. . . . and also learning a little bit about the library 'cause at an academic library, you know, the process is also part of, I think, what they should learn here.

D. Sample Negative Librarian Incident
Librarian Negative Incident - #7
Librarian (L08) Relational—Negative User Attitude toward Librarian (User Impatient)
L08. *Yes,* {laugh} it was a young woman who came in and wanted information about statehood and Puerto Rico. It took a while to even get to that point because of her accent, and each time I would suggest some-

thing, she said, well, she already knew it or she had done it, and also it was one of those interviews where she kept jumping in each time I made a suggestion. And we finally got to a point but it was frustrating because she seemed to think that I was either not attempting to help her or that I was asking too many questions. And when I finally I think what I had to tell her was she had to first of all have some background about what Puerto Rico was like and *why* they wanted statehood, not just to jump in and say I need the information on statehood alone and nothing else. But it was *frustrating*.

I. Um hum.

L08. I did get to the point where she did understand that she needed a little bit more about the background . . .

I. Um hum.

L08. . . . about why the Puerto Ricans wanted statehood.

I. So again, can you put your finger do you think, to tell me *exactly* what it was that made it frustrating or unsuccessful?

L08. I think the frustration was that she, I'm not sure whether she was listening or not or whether she had thoughts of her own, but she kept interrupting each time I, *almost* each time I, I shouldn't say each time, but frequently interrupted whenever I had a question as to exactly what it was she wanted and perhaps this is what we ought to do.

I. So she was, like, impatient?

L08. Impatient and also, yeah, maybe impatient with me, as if to say I didn't quite understand what it was that . . .

I. Um hum.

L08. . . . she might really be searching for.

I. Um hum.

L08. . . . and now when I did give her information we found, I left her at the computer for a while and I went and she was gone, and I said, "Oh there was an *excellent* article I just came upon, did you take that information?" It was from the *New York Times Magazine* which is always a good, *almost* always a good source {laugh} and she said, "Oh no, no." She really didn't have the time. So that was also frustrating as if she did not really have the time to do it at that moment.

I. Um hum.

L08. And she said, "I'll come back." And I don't know whether or not she did, but she knew it was there if she wanted it.

Appendix G

Outline of Categories

❦❧ ❦❧ ❦❧ ❦❧ ❦❧ ❦❧ ❦❧ ❦❧ ❦❧

I. Goals or Aims of the Interaction
  A. Librarian Goals
    1. Problem definition (9L)
        a. Defining, clarifying user's goal (8L)
        b. Surface structure versus deep structure (5L)
        c. Defining user's background and current state (4L)
        d. Help user understand assignment (2L)
        e. Help user reformulate problem (1L)
        f. Determining amount of information needed (1L)
    2. Developing strategies for solving the problem (7L)
        a. Assist user in finding information (4L)
        b. Information delivery (3L)
        c. Determine possible expansion areas for research (3L)
        d. Answer the question (3L)
        e. Referral (2L)
        f. Help user formulate differing approaches (2L)
        g. Get user started in right direction (2L)
        h. Help user complete assignment (1L)
        i. Information access (1L)
    3. Enablement (6L)
        a. Help user become independent in finding information (5L)
        b. To educate the user (2L)

       c. Help user learn to evaluate the information or source of information (2L)

       d. Help user understand information systems (1L)

       e. Help user understand organization of libraries (1L)

       f. Stretch user intellectually (1L)

    4. Developing positive attitude toward library program (1L)

    5. Gaining user's confidence (1L)

    6. Composite of above goals (3L)

    7. Goal dependent upon context of question

       a. Varies by type of library (2L)

       b. Varies by type of user (2L)

       c. Varies by type of question (1L)

  B. User Goals

    1. Developing strategies for solving the problem (26U)

       a. To find someone to assist, help, give direction in finding information (15U)

       b. Information access, to find information (13U)

       c. To get started (4U)

       d. Find information in the fastest way (2U)

       e. To make the librarian understand, listen to need (2U)

       f. Information delivery (2U)

       g. To find out various options (2U)

       h. To get the right answer (2U)

       i. To find a book (1U)

       j. To get a referral (1U)

       k. To pinpoint sources, zero in (1U)

    2. Enablement, to help become independent (2U)

    3. Goal depends on context (1U)

II. Facilitators: Qualitities That Enhance Goals, Communication

  A. Librarian's perception of user characteristics that facilitate goal achievement

    1. Content factors

       a. Knowledge base (7L)

         i. General knowledge (5L)

           (a) Intellectually suited, bright (4L)

           (b) Able to comprehend (3L)

(c) Possess broad knowledge (2L)

(d) Have good language skills (2L)

(e) Ability to follow directions (1L)

(f) Knowledge of English language (1L)

(g) Organized thoughts (1L)

(h) Quickly apply learning (i.e., computer searching) (1L)

ii. Specialized knowledge (5L)

(a) Knowledge of library science

(i) Understands research process (2L)

(ii) Overall sense of how the library works (1L)

(b) Knowledge of information need

(i) Know exactly what they are looking for (2L)

(ii) Planned how to approach question (1L)

(iii) State what they are looking for (2L)

2. Relational Factors

a. Attitude (10L)

i. Positive attitude toward librarians, positive history (3L)

ii. Positive attitude toward task (10L)

(a) Serious (2L)

(b) Motivated (2L)

(c) Assertive (2L)

(d) Persistent (2L)

(e) Patient (2L)

(f) Has realistic expectations (2L)

(g) Confident (1L)

b. Relationship quality (10L)

i. Enthusiastic, interested in learning, curious (8L)

ii. Good communication skills (2L)

(a) Willing to self-disclose, openness (3L)

(b) Honest, direct (2L)

(c) Good listener (1L)

(d) Not defensive, apologizing for question (1L)

(e) Responsive (1L)

(f) Trusts the librarian (1L)

(i) In confidential matter (1L)

(ii) Uncomfortable topics (1L)

iii. Accepts help from librarian (4L)

   (a) Accepts authority of librarian (3L)
   (b) Recognizes that librarian is there to help (2L)
iv. Process oriented (8L)
   (a) Willing to give enough time (3L)
   (b) Takes responsibility to ask for more help if needed (3L)
   (c) Determined to accomplish goal (1L)
   (d) Not afraid to dig in (1L)
   (e) Proactive (1L)
   (f) Can handle options for search (1L)
B. Librarian's perceptions of librarian characteristics that facilitate goal achievement
   1. Content factors
      a. Knowledge base (11L)
         i. General Knowledge (4L)
            (a) Broad liberal arts foundation, broad general knowledge (2L)
            (b) Has analytic skills (2L)
            (c) Has a multicultural background (1L)
         ii. Specialized knowledge (11L)
            (a) Subject knowledge (3L)
               (i) Knowledge of subject of question (3L)
               (ii) Holds subject master's degree (1L)
            (b) Library knowledge (8L)
               (i) Can think of different options (3L)
               (ii) Knowledge of library collection (3L)
               (iii) Holds master,s in library science (1L)
               (iv)Knowledge of structure of information (1L)
               (v) Experienced (1L)
               (vi)Keeping current with advances in the field (1L)
               (vii) Asks the right questions(1L)
            (c) Knowledge of tools, information sources (4L)
      b. Information access, ability to network with other librarians (1L)
   2. Relational factors
      a. Attitude of librarian (9L)
         i. Positive attitude toward user (5L)

(a) Patient (2L)

(b) Friendly (1L)

(c) Reassuring (1L)

(d) Sweet (1L)

(e) Treats people equally (1L)

(f) Empathetic, sympathetic (1L)

(g) Remains objective and free of hostility (e.g., with problem user) (1L)

(h) Able to set priorities (e.g., phone, line of users) (1L)

ii. Positive attitude toward task (6L)

(a) Curious about everything (3L)

(b) Genuinely interested in working with people (2L)

(c) Identifies with user, takes queries as own (2L)

(d) Has perseverance (1L)

(e) Likes what they are doing (1L)

(f) Enjoys teaching people (1L)

(g) Professional (1L)

(h) Likes people (1L)

(i) Excited, dynamic (1L)

b. Relationship quality (9L)

i. Good communication skills (3L)

(a) Good listener (5L)

(b) Intuitive (4L)

(c) Good people skills (3L)

(d) Able to read people, catch social cues easily (3L)

(e) Flexible, sensitive to situation (being humorous or serious as the occasion merits) (3L)

(f) Receptive and open (2L)

(g) Ability to make the user feel comfortable (2L)

(h) Builds rapport (1L)

(i) Gives verbal encouragement (1L)

(j) Digests user's need quickly (1L)

(k) Thinks quickly (1L)

ii. Process oriented (6L)

(a) Invites user to return if additional help is needed (1L)

(b) Takes time to explain sources and systems (1L)

(c) Willing to give extra help to those who need it, coddles user (1L)

(d) Motivates user to dig more (1L)

(e) Does not overload users with information (1L)

(f) Helps users "avoid hassles," steers them through system (1L)

(g) Nurtures users (1L)

c. Approachability (3L)

   i. Exhibits positive nonverbal behavior (1L)

      (a) Looks people in the eye (1L)

      (b) Nods (1L)

      (c) Leans forward (1L)

      (d) Smiles (1L)

   ii. Not stuck to the desk (1L)

C. User's perceptions of librarian characteristics that facilitate goal achievement

1. Content factors

   a. Information related (18U)

      i. Information delivery (6U)

         (a) Gives efficient, quick service(2U)

         (b) Specific (1U)

      ii. Information access (3U)

         (a) Is an information advocate, does whatever's necessary to help user gain access to needed information (2U)

         (b) Makes referral (2U)

      iii. Filling information need (11U)

         (a) Accompanies user to source (8U)

         (b) Makes sure user finds information (4U)

         (c) Thorough (3U)

      iv. Product oriented (2U)

         (a) Helps to expand topic (1U)

         (b) Gives opinions on how to complete assignment in addition to information (1U)

   b. Knowledge base (11U)

      i. Specialized knowledge (2U)

    (a) Knowing how to help even if not knowledgeable in subject (1U)

    (b) Resourceful (1U)

  ii. Knowledge of information retrieval tools (9U)

    (a) Knowledge of sources, materials (9U)

    (b) Current with new sources (2U)

2. Relational factors

  a. Attitude (2U)

    i. Positive attitude toward user (23U)

      (a) Helpful (17U)

      (b) Pleasant, nice (10U)

      (c) Friendly (4U)

      (d) Patient (3U)

      (e) Attentive to user needs, caring (3U)

      (f) Respectful, courteous (3U)

      (g) Understanding (1U)

      (h) Cooperative (1U)

      (i) Does not question user's need for help (1U)

    ii. Positive attitude toward task (8U)

      (a) Interested in helping (8U)

      (b) Enjoys job (1U)

      (c) Persistent (1U)

      (d) Professional (1U)

  b. Relationship quality (16U)

    i. Good communication skills (1U)

      (a) Personable (3U)

      (b) Makes user feel comfortable (2U)

      (c) Receptive (1U)

      (d) Sense of humor (1U)

      (e) Rapport building, previous interactions (1U)

    ii. Enthusiastic (2U)

    iii. Process oriented (13U)

      (a) Takes time to explain systems and sources (9U)

      (b) Makes extra effort to help user (4U)

      (c) Willing to work together with user (1U)

      (d) Makes sure user understands what to do (1U)

    c. Approachability (2U)

       i. Gives nonverbal acknowledgment (i.e., eye contact) (1U)

      ii. Gets up from behind desk (1U)

D. Perceptions of information technologies as facilitators to goal achievement

  1. Librarian perceptions

    a. Content factors (11L)

       i. Impact on search process (9L)

         (a) Easier to find information (6L)

         (b) Need to teach both how to search and subject access (4L)

         (c) Increased breadth and depth of information (2L)

         (d) Increased options (1L)

         (e) Increased efficiency of search (1L)

         (f) Utilizes subject knowledge plus computer knowledge (1L)

         (g) Users get more complete information (1L)

      ii. Impact on information retrieval (3L)

         (a) Increased accessibility through networks (2L)

         (b) Users get faster retrieval (1L)

         (c) Increased amount of information available on computer (1L)

    b. Relational factors, impact of technology on relationship (9L)

       i. Labor-intensive, interacting more, increased role (4L)

      ii. Users comfortable with computers (3L)

      iii. Effect on basic interaction

         (a) Not affected basic interaction (2L)

         (b) Changed entire interaction (1L)

      iv. Effect on duration of interaction

         (a) Increased time (3L)

         (b) Spend less time with user (1L)

         (c) Amount of time spent varies with context of interaction (1L)

         (d) Different kind of time (1L)

      v. More exciting for user (2L)

vi. Some users learn it on their own (1L)

vii. Reduces user frustration (1L)

2. User perceptions

a. Content factors (4U)

i. Librarian knowledgeable about computerized systems (2U)

ii. Librarian demonstrates how to work computer (2U)

iii. Computer is big time-saver (1U)

b. Relational factor, computer is fun (1U)

III. Barriers: Characteristics That Impede Goals, Communication

A. Librarian's perception of user characteristics that are barriers to goal achievement

1. Content

a. Knowledge base (7L)

i. General knowledge, has language barrier, international students (1L)

ii. Specialized knowledge (6L)

(a) Library knowledge (2L)

(i) Ignorant of the basic library structure (2L)

(ii) Lacks understanding of the research process (1L)

(iii) Has had no library training (1L)

(b) Lack of knowledge about information need (5L)

(i) Does not understand assignment (3L)

(ii) Not prepared (2L)

(iii) Has incorrect or incomplete information (2L)

(iv) Does not know what they want (1L)

(v) Gives librarian too much information (1L)

(c) Inability to articulate need (4L)

(i) Asks general questions when wanting specific answers (1L)

(ii) Articulates need inappropriately (1L)

2. Relational factors

a. Negative attitude (8L)

i. Negative attitude toward librarian (8L)

(a) Impatient (6L)

     (b) Fearful, timid (4L)
         (i) Fears looking stupid (5L)
         (ii) Fears bothering librarian (1L)
         (iii) Sees librarian as threat, authority figure (1L)
         (iv) Fears institution (2L)
     (c) Insecure, helpless, acutely dependent (4L)
     (d) Angry, hostile (3L)
     (e) Arrogant (2L)
     (f) Obnoxious, nasty (2L)
     (g) Holds negative preconceptions about librarian (1L)
         (i) Negative history (1L, 1U)
         (ii) Expects librarian not to care (1L)
         (iii) Expects librarian to be unprofessional (1L)
         (iv) Expects to be frustrated (1L)
     (h) Closed-minded (1L)
     (i) Disrespectful (1L)
  ii. Negative attitude toward task (5L)
     (a) Resentful (4L)
         (i) Resents library assignment (3L)
         (ii) Resents being queried (1L)
         (iii) Resents library policy (1L)
     (b) Reluctant (2L)
     (c) Not interested (2L)
     (d) Not serious about studies (1L)
 b. Relationship quality (10L)
   i. User rejects librarian (7L)
     (a) Disregards information given by librarian (5L)
     (b) Does not permit librarian to help (1L)
     (c) Interrupts (1L)
  ii. User lacks self-disclosure (4L)
     (a) Surrogate—doing someone else's work (3L)
     (b) Disguised question—pretense of being more knowl-
         edgeable (1L)
     (c) Disguised question- sensitive subject such as job
         search, medical question (3L)
  iii. Poor communication skills (2L)
     (a) Inattentive (2L)

    (b) Lacks people skills (1L)

  iv. Not process oriented (6L)

    (a) Looks for easiest way to complete assignment and get out (4L)

    (b) Waits until the last minute to do assignment, procrastinates (3L)

    (c) Does not want to spend necessary time (3L)

    (d) Overly concerned with final product rather than learning process (2L)

    (e) Not understanding that librarian needs information to make interaction successful (1L)

    (f) Expects to be handed everything (1L)

    (g) Unwilling to learn (1L)

B. Librarian's perception of librarian characteristics that are barriers to goal achievement

  1. Content factors

    a. Knowledge base (5L)

      i. Specialized knowledge (3L)

      (a). Poor grasp of subject of query (2L)

      (b). Doesn't know collection (1L)

      ii. Inexperienced (1L)

      iii. Unprepared (1L)

      iv. Not up to date (1L)

      v. Knowledge of information retrieval tools (3L)

      (a) Poor grasp of electronic sources (3L)

      (b) Unfamiliar with specialized sources, especially business and legal (1L)

  2. Relational factors

    a. Negative attitude (8L)

      i. Negative attitude toward user (6L)

      (a) Unresponsive, cold (2L)

      (b) Insecure, threatened by the question (2L)

      (c) Forbidding (1L)

      (d) Prejudiced (1L)

        (i) Racist (1L)

        (ii) Ageist (1L)

      (e) Treats user as helpless (1L)

(f) Condescending (1L)

(g) Rides roughshod over users (1L)

(h) Treats user or question as unimportant (1L)

(i) Rude (1L)

(j) Avoids user (1L)

    (i) Shy, private, (1L)

    (ii) Became librarian to hide (1L)

ii. Negative attitude toward task (7L)

(a) Impatient (3L)

(b) Lacks pride in profession (2L)

(c) Lazy (1L)

(d) Uninterested (1L)

(e) Does not like what they are doing (1L)

(f) Unnerved by pressure (1L)

(g) Not motivated (1L)

iii. Physically attracted to user (1L)

b. Relationship quality (7L)

i. Poor communication skills (4L)

(a) Monotone presentation (1L)

(b) Lacks people skills (1L)

(c) Overly enthusiastic (1L)

(d) Interrupts waiting users with phone reference questions (1L)

(e) Eccentric (1L)

(f) Unprofessional (1L)

ii. Not process oriented (5L)

(a) Not persistent (3L)

(b) Gives minimal help, points (3L)

(c) Not willing to invest time (2L)

(d) Gives answer without teaching the process (1L)

c. Approachability (3L)

i. Negative nonverbal behavior (1L)

(a) Points (2L)

(b) Does not move (1L)

(c) Does not nod (1L)

(d) Does not look receptive (1L)

        (e)   Has body language that tells user you're crazy or stupid (1L)

        (f)   Stares (1L)

     ii. Avoids user contact (1L)

C. User's perception of librarian characteristics that are barriers to goal achievement

   1. Content

      a. Information related (1U)

        i. Lack of information delivery, tries to substitute inappropriate or unwanted material to pacify user (1U)

      b. Knowledge base (2U)

        i. Specialized knowledge (2U)

          (a) Lacks subject knowledge (1U)

          (b)   Lacks knowledge of computerized systems (1U)

   2. Relational factors

      a. Negative attitude (10U)

        i. Negative attitude toward user (9L)

          (a) Evades user (4U)

             (i) Not wanting to get involved (2U)

             (ii) Does not take user's request seriously (1U)

             (iii) Questions user's need for help (1U)

          (b) Resists user (4U)

             (i) Impatient (2U)

             (ii) Puritanical, refusing to do "user's work" (1U)

             (iii) Sour (1U)

             (iv) Not caring about what user wants (1U)

             (v) Cold (1U)

          (c)   Resists interaction (4U)

             (i) Has had a bad day (3U)

             (ii) Has personality conflict (2U)

             (iii) Stressed out (2U)

        ii. Negative attitude toward task (6U)

          (a)   Begrudging attitude, acting as if request is inconvenient (5U)

          (b)   Not interested (1U)

          (c)   Does not want to be librarian (1U)

b. Poor relationship quality (9U)
  i. Poor communication skills (7U)
    (a) Shows disrespect, rude (4U)
    (b) Abrupt (3U)
    (c) Comes on strong, belittles user (2U)
    (d) Condescending (1U)
    (e) Sarcastic (1U)
    (f) Elicits defensive behavior from user (1U)
    (g) Not intuitive (1U)
  ii. Not process oriented (5U)
    (a) Gives minimalist help, answers surface question (4U)
    (b) Not willing to give time to help (3U)
    (c) Reluctant to search for material not readily available (2U)
c. Lack of approachability (15U)
  i. Has negative nonverbal behaviors (12U)
    (a) Points rather than shows user to source (4U)
    (b) Distracted, inattentive, preoccupied (4U)
    (c) Negative paralanguage: sigh, moaning, groaning, tone of voice (3U)
    (d) Negative facial, eye expression, blank stare (3U)
    (e) Sits, does not get up from desk (3U)
    (f) Looks annoyed (2U)
    (g) Lacks eye contact (2U)
    (h) Eats or drinks (1U)
    (i) Talks to somebody (1U)
    (j) Not smiling (1U)
    (k) Watches clock (1U)
D. User's perceptions of user's characteristics that are barriers to goal achievement.
  1. Content factors (1U)
    a. Lack of knowledge base, systems related, uncomfortable with computers (1U)
  2. Relational factors
    a. Negative attitude toward librarian (3U)
      i. Fears looking stupid (2U)
      ii. Has poor attitude, wiseass (1U)

          iii. Fears library, librarian (1U)

      b. Negative attitude toward task (2U)

          i. Wants to get resources and get out (1U)

          ii. Procrastinates, leaves things for the last minute (1U)

E. Perceptions of information retrieval technologies as barriers

  1. Librarian's perceptions

      a. Content factors (7L)

          i. Negative impact on search process (4L)

            (a) Makes users want more and more (1L)

            (b) Strains librarian resources, takes more time, more users, less librarians (1L)

            (c) Computer terminals unavailable, being used (2L)

            (d) Changed entire interaction, more intensive (1L)

          ii. Negative impact on information retrieval (2L)

            (a) Users inaccurate with retrieval (1L)

            (b) Even users who are computer smart don't understand how to search (1L)

          iii. Negative impact of maintenance routines (4L)

            (a) Provides librarians with administrative burden (hardware and software support) (2L)

            (b) Needs to deal with technological breakdown (2L)

      b. Relational factors (3L)

          i. Fosters user dependence on librarian (1L)

          ii. Made reference interview more difficult, increased user expectations (e.g., full text) (2L)

  2. User's perceptions

      a. Content (3U)

          i. Librarian uncomfortable with computers (2U)

          ii. Librarian lacks knowledge of computerized systems (1U)

          iii. Librarian resists technological change (1U)

          iv. Computer hardware may malfunction (1U)

          v. User uncomfortable with computers (1U)

F. External constraints that form barriers to goal achievement

  1. Lack of time (7L,4U)

  2. Lack of resources (8L,1U)

      a. Materials in collection, but missing from shelves (2L)

      b. Information available only in foreign language (1L)

    c. Material too difficult for user (1L)

    d. No information available, poor assignment (1L)

3. Distracting level of activity in library (5L,2U)

    a. Busy, line of users waiting (3L,2U)

    b. Phone ringing (3L)

    c. Number of librarians on duty (1L)

    d. Interruptions (1L)

4. Uncomfortable physical facility, environment (1L,2U)

    a. Library hot and stuffy (1U)

    b. Physical arrangement of sources poor (1L)

    c. Noisy, no quiet study area (1U)

Appendix H

Terminology

❀ ❀ ❀ ❀ ❀ ❀ ❀ ❀ ❀

Academic library: A library forming an integral part of a college, university, or other academic institution for postsecondary education, organized and administered to meet the information needs of students, faculty, and affiliated staff of the institution.[1]

Library user: A person who uses library materials or services. Preferred to the term *reader*, because library collections include materials that may be read, viewed, or listened to, and to the term *patron*, which denotes a library advocate or supporter.[2]

Reference interview: The interpersonal communication between a reference staff member and a library user to determine the precise information needs of the user. Synonymous with question negotiation.[3]

Reference librarian: A librarian employed in a reference department or responsible for providing information service.[4]

Reference question: Any request by a library user for information or assistance in locating information which involves an encounter in person, by mail, by telephone, or by other means between the user and a member of the reference staff.[5]

Notes

1. Heartsill Young, ed. *The ALA Glossary of Library and Information Science* (Chicago: ALA, 1983), 1.

2. Ibid., 132.

3. Ibid., 188.

4. Ibid., 188.

5. Ibid., 188.

Appendix I

Sample Paired Perception
Interview Transcripts

∻ ∻ ∻ ∻ ∻ ∻ ∻ ∻ ∻

A. Interview U06 about L06

I. Okay, a few minutes ago, you asked the reference librarian for help. Could you please tell me what happened . . . . describe what happened?

U06. I requested books on Rush. I'm doing a research paper at school and I wanted materials about the band and books that they used to get the lyrics.

I. Okay.

U06. So she pointed me in the direction.

I. How do you think that went?

U06. Well, so far, I, I've found a little bit. I haven't finished reading, but it should go okay.

I. Okay, did you get the help that you needed?

U06. To this point, yeah.

I. Yeah? Okay.

U06. I'll have to see when I finish reading.

I. Okay. If you needed help again, would you ask the same person for help and could you tell me why?

U06. She's helpful.

I. She's helpful?

U06. Yeah, she helped me.

I. Yeah. What do you mean by helpful? Can you talk about that?

U06. She was willing to go out of her way to help me, ah, gave me more information than I needed, I think.[1]

I. Okay, so then was this a useful discussion for you?

U06. Yeah.[2]

I. What, what, for you, are your goals or your aims when you ask a librarian for help?

U06. They're gonna give me what I need, help me as much as possible.

I. Okay. Are you, do you, um, usually try to find stuff on your own before you . . . ?

U06. Yeah, usually I try [something unintelligible].

I. Okay. In this case, did you try to find stuff on your own first?

U06. Yeah, but I'm not familiar with this library.

I. Okay. Could you think back over other times when you've asked a librarian for help. Can you think of a time that was a really successful interaction, one that you think went really well? Can you describe it for me?

U06. It, it's pretty much minor things that I need help with.

I. Okay. Was there ever a time when you asked a librarian for help, and it was unsuccessful or negative?

U06. Yeah. I requested several books a couple weeks ago, and they never came in so I went to see where they were and they never followed it up to see where they were. So they sent me back.

I. Okay. What about that was really negative for you?

U06. The fact that they didn't contact me to see if the books were already borrowed. So I was waiting for them to come and they never arrived.

I. Okay.

U06. I was not notified.

I. When you went, did you then talk to the librarian to find out what the problem was?

U06. Yeah.

I. And what happened then?

U06. Ah, she just, she suggested that trying different method, she didn't try and locate the books at all.

I. Was she nice about it?

U06. She didn't look too concerned about it.

I. So you got the impression she didn't really care.

U06. Yeah.

I. She wasn't really . . . so, for you what exactly was it that made that unsuccessful? Was it the attitude?

U06. Yeah, her attitude. She didn't care about what I wanted.

I. Was that worse than not getting the books? How she treated you?

U06. Yeah, definitely.

I. Okay, okay. How would you have changed that interaction if you could, the one you were just talking about that was unsuccessful?

U06. I don't know.

I. Okay, okay, very good. Let's stop.

B. Interview L06 about U06

I. Would you please just describe the whole interaction? What happened?

L06. Okay. He came up with a question about . . . finding articles I think it was about Rush, about Rush's lyrics . . . and he had apparently looked in the catalog and not found anything in the [site B] catalog . . . and I was somewhat at a loss because you know, frankly I {fake cough} I mean I may have *heard* of this group before, but I certainly never listened to any of their music, you know.

I. I haven't either. So.

L06. No idea. But then he kind of led a little bit further and said that he was looking for, like, literary allusions that they had made and then he showed me an entry of a book that, um, he knew that they had made allusions to, and it was Ayn Rand

I. Oh.

L06. Yeah. *Fountainhead,* and apparently, they, he, they had also used *Anthem* so I had some sense that these were not the kinds of literary allusions that they were making were not *Catcher in the Rye* type things but . . .

I. Or even biblical. I mean, a lot of them are biblical.

L06. Yeah, yeah, but apparently, and then so I asked him to bring over the lyrics which he had with me. So I looked at those, so in the lyrics they were referring to a lot of classical mythology plus the Rand-ish references. So we talked about coming at it from two directions. One is coming at it through the music, sort of the music focus I didn't think a general index would be much good but it turned out we did have *Music Index* and we went schleping over there and we found in the first volume that I pulled out a few entries for Rush and . . . you know, I advised him that he'd probably want to go through a few of them, of the indexes, that they would have more . . . {something unintelligible}

I. Right.

L06. . . . garbage and . . . then, we then we talked about coming at it from the literary standpoint and I took him over to the dictionaries of literary allusions and that kind of thing because I did think with the kind of classical things that he was coming up with that he would probably find something there. And then *he* said bright cookie, "But my friend said that he got something on a computer," Oh okay, so that led naturally into *MLA.*

I. Um.

L06. So we talked a little bit about searching *MLA,* and I think at that point I sort of recapped, you know, coming at it from music, coming at it from lit. crit. and I sort of left him to it . . .

I. Um hum.

L06. . . . at that point.

I. Um hum. So how do you think this one went? {laugh}

L06. *That one* {shared laughter} I think went *much* better I was *much* happier with that one; it wasn't a standard information question. It, there wasn't an *answer* that we were looking for. It was a process that we were that we were kind of going through, and I think it sort of fun when you can lead people towards, um, thinking of more than one approach to a question.

I. Um hum.

L06. Yeah, that, that's kind of interesting, and he was willing to do that.

I. Um hum.

L06. Yeah, so I just think it went more smoothly. I think I'm better at the process questions . . .

I. Um hum.

L06. . . . than I am at the straight answer {laugh} ones.

I. {something unintelligible} But, so what was important to you in this interaction then, your . . . ?

L06. First, making sure that I understood . . .

I. Um hum.

L06. . . . where he was really coming from 'cause otherwise I wouldn't have wanted to not being familiar with the group that he was looking at. I needed to have some sense {laugh} of what direction to go in with that.

I. Right.

L06. So knowing where he was coming from was important to getting him to think about, um, differing approaches to the question . . .

I. Um hum.

L06. . . . was important, and getting him to indexes and sources that would sort of lead, that would actually come up with some information for him.

I. Um hum.

L06. Yeah.

I. Um hum. Okay. Do you think the user got the help that they wanted, that he wanted?

L06. I think so. I think he still got more work to do in terms of actually gathering the information, and I think he might have been more comfortable had I been able to locate an article on "Literary Allusions in the in Rush Lyrics," . . .

I. Right, right.

L06. . . . you know, and I don't think he was real comfortable with that ambiguity. But discomfort is part of the process so, you know, I don't think he was totally satisfied but . . . I'm comfortable with the tension in which I left it.

I. Okay.

L06. It's kind of . . . it's a sort of a manipulative thing to say, but you know, yeah, you can't take it all away.

I. Right, right. So then how did this interaction measure up? Would you have changed anything if you could go back and do it again?

L06. I might have helped him with the *MLA* CD, you know, actually physically taken him, you know, gotten it and gotten him set up and ready to go. But I think that would be about the only thing that I could change, yeah, yeah.

I. I don't think that he was really ready for that frankly, that literary allusions if he . . .

L06. . . . to get some sense of what kind of things he can expect and then to get into the electronic . . .

I. . . . 'cause he felt, in fact, I could just share this with you after talking with him about he was really happy with the interaction, but he felt that it was too much, you know, almost too much information at once.

L06. It gets hard, it gets hard to . . .

I. But also you didn't know that he's a high school student either, so . . .

L06. Yeah.

I. You were . . .

L06. Um hum.

I. . . . he looked like a high school, like a college student.

L06. Yeah, I was figuring first year.

I. Yeah, so you were probably operating a little bit above . . .

L06. Which is okay.

I. . . . his level, but that's okay.

L06. I don't have a problem.

I. He handled it really well.

L06. Yeah, I don't have a problem . . .

I. Yeah.

L06. . . . with doing that either.

I. It's better, I think, than going the other way.

L06. I'd rather stretch . . .

I. Yeah.

L06. . . . particularly at that age, . . .

I. Yeah.

L06. . . . and then make it too.

I. I think that's, you're very, have good insight when you said he probably would have been happier if you would have been able to give him an article on, 'cause I think he's not comfortable . . .

L06. . . . he's not comfortable with the ambiguity, and I don't think he realizes yet that the ambiguity is part of the process.

I. Right. But I mean he's probably also, he's a naive user that they come in and think that I'm doing a paper on [there's gotta be lots of articles on this topic . . .

L06. . . . this is a college library, there's lots of stuff, lots of stuff. Yeah, yeah. {shared laugh}.

I. Okay.

L06. Actually, I was getting kind of excited about it because it looked like he was going to be doing something kind of original that I had been feeling was within his grasp. Which is kind of exciting.

I. So this one for you was real successful.

L06. Much more so, yes. Yeah.

I. Let's stop.

Notes

1. He thought the librarian gave more information than was needed. The librarian, on the other hand, if asked what would she change if she had to go back, thought she should have shown another source in detail, more information yet.

2. This was like pulling teeth. I could have pushed here but I didn't think it was worth it

Bibliography

Allen, Mary Beth, "International Students in Academic Libraries: A User Survey," *College & Research Libraries* 54 (July 1993): 323–33.

Andersson, Bengt-Erik, and Nilsson, Stig-Goran, "Studies in the Reliability and Validity of the Critical Incident Technique," *Journal of Applied Psychology* 48 (1964): 398–403.

Anthes, Susan H., "High Tech/High Touch: Academic Libraries Respond to Change in the Behavioral Sciences," *Behavioral & Social Sciences Librarian* 5 (fall 1985): 53–65.

Awaritefe, Milena, "Psychology Applied to Librarianship," *International Library Review* 16 (Jan. 1984): 27–33.

Baker, Sharon L., and Lancaster, Frederick Wilfred, *The Measurement and Evaluation of Library Services,* 2nd ed. (Arlington, Va.: Information Resources Pr., 1991).

Bailey, Bill, "The Personal Librarian," *Library Journal* 109 (Oct. 1, 1984): 1820–21.

Bailey, William G., "The '55 Percent Rule' Revisited," *Journal of Academic Librarianship* 13 (Nov. 1987): 280–82.

Bearman, Toni Carbo, ed., "Educating the Future Information Professional," *Library-Hi-Tech* 5 (summer 1987): 27–40.

Bechtel, Joan M., "Conversation: A New Paradigm for Librarianship?" *College & Research Libraries* 47 (May 1986): 219–24.

Belkin, Nicholas J., Oddy, Robert N., and Brooks, Helen M., "ASK for Information Retrieval, Part I: Background and Theory," *Journal of Documentation* 38 (June 1982): 61–71.

Belkin, Nicholas J., Oddy, Robert N., and Brooks, Helen M., "ASK for Information Retrieval, Part II: Results of a Design Study," *Journal of Documentation* 38 (Sept. 1982): 145–64.

Benham, Frances, and Powell, Ronald R., *Success in Answering Reference Questions: Two Studies.* (Metuchen, N.J.: Scarecrow, 1987).

Berger, Charles R., and diBattista, Patrick, "Information Seeking and Plan Elaboration: What Do You Need to Know to Know What To Do?" *Communication Monographs* 59 (Dec. 1992): 368–87.

Berlo, David K., *The Process of Communication.* (New York: Holt, 1960).

Berscheid, Ellen, "Interpersonal Attraction," in *Handbook of Social Psychology,* Vol. 2. 3rd ed., ed. by Gardner Lindzey and Elliot Aronson (New York: Random House, 1985), 413–84.

Berscheid, Ellen, and Hatfield, Elaine, *Interpersonal Attraction*, 2nd ed. (Reading, Mass.: Addison-Wesley, 1978).

Bessler, Joanne M., *Putting Service into Library Staff Training* (Chicago: ALA, 1994).

Birbeck, Vaughan P., "Unobtrusive Testing of Public Library Reference Service," *Refer* 4 (1986): 5–9.

Black, Sandra M., "Personality—Librarians as Communicators," *Canadian Library Journal* 38 (Apr. 1981): 65–71.

Boucher, Virginia, "Nonverbal Communication and the Library Reference Interview," *RQ* 16 (fall 1976): 27–32.

Bradley, Jana, "Methodological Issues and Practices in Qualitative Research," *Library Quarterly* 63 (Oct. 1993): 431–49.

Brewer, John, and Hunter, Albert, *Multimethod Research: A Synthesis of Styles* (Newbury Park, Calif.: Sage, 1989).

Budd, John M., "A Critique of Customer and Commodity," *College & Research Libraries* 58 (July 1997): 310–21.

———, "User-Centered Thinking: Lessons from Reader-Centered Theory," *RQ* 34 (summer 1995): 487–96.

———, *The Library and Its Users: The Communication Process.* (Westport, Conn.: Greenwood Pr., 1992).

———, "The User and the Library: A Discussion of Communication," *Reference Librarian,* no. 20 (1987): 205–21.

Budd, Richard W., "Review of *The Measurement and Evaluation of Library Service* by Sharon L. Baker and F. Wilfrid Lancaster," *Library Quarterly* 62 (Oct. 1992): 461–62.

Bunge, Charles A., "Interpersonal Dimensions of the Reference Interview: A Historical Review of the Literature," *Drexel Library Quarterly* 20 (spring 1984): 4–23.

Burgoon, Judee K., Buller, David B., and Woodall, W. Gill. *Nonverbal Communication: The Unspoken Dialogue* (New York: Harper & Row, 1989).

Burgoon, Judee K., and Hale, Jerold L., "The Fundamental Topoi of Relational Communication," *Communication Monographs* 51 (Sept. 1984): 193–214.

Burke, Kenneth, *A Grammar of Motives* (New York: Prentice Hall, 1952).

Chelton, Mary Kathleen, "Adult-Adolescent Service Encounters: The Library Context" (Ph.D. diss., Rutgers—State Univ. of New Jersey, 1997).

Childers, Thomas, "The Quality of Reference: Still Moot after 20 Years," *Journal of Academic Librarianship* 13 (May 1987): 73–74.

Crouch, Wayne W., *The Information Interview: a Comprehensive Bibliography and an Analysis of the Literature* (Washington D.C.: National Institute of Education [DHEW], 1979). ERIC Document 180 501.

Cummins, Thompson. R., "Question Clarification in the Reference Encounter," *Canadian Library Journal* 41 (Apr. 1984): 63–67.

Denzin, Norman K., *Sociological Methods: A Sourcebook* (Chicago: Aldine, 1970).

Dervin, Brenda, "Useful Theory for Librarianship: Communication, Not Information," *Drexel Library Quarterly* 13 (July 1977): 16–32.

Dervin, Brenda, and Dewdney, Patricia, "Neutral Questioning: A New Approach to the Reference Interview," *RQ* 25 (summer 1986): 506–13.

Deutsch, Morton, "An Experimental Study of the Effects of Co-operation and Completion upon Group Process," *Human Relations* 2 (July 1949): 199–231.

DeVore-Chew, Marynelle, Roberts, Brian, and Smith, Nathan M., "The Effects of Reference Librarians' Nonverbal Communications on the Patrons' Perceptions of the Library, Librarians, and Themselves," *Library and Information Science Research* 10 (Oct.–Dec. 1988): 389–400.

Dewdney, Patricia, "The Effects of Training Reference Librarians in Interview Skills: A Field Experiment" (Ph.D. diss., School of Library and Information Service, Univ. of Western Ontario, 1986).

Dewdney, Patricia, and Michell, Gillian, "Oranges and Peaches: Understanding Communication Accidents in the Reference Interview," *RQ* 35 (summer 1996): 520–36.

Dewdney, Patricia, and Ross, Catherine Sheldrick, "Flying a Light Aircraft: Reference Service Evaluation from the User's Viewpoint," *RQ* 34 (winter 1994): 217–30.

Durrance, Joan C., "Reference Success: Does the 55 Percent Rule Tell the Whole Story?" *Library Journal* 114 (Apr., 1989): 31–36.

Edwards, Susan, and Browne, Mairead, "Quality in Information Services: Do Users and Librarians Differ in Their Expectations?" *Library and Information Science Research* 17 (spring 1995): 163–82.

Eichman, Thomas Lee, "The Complex Nature of Opening Reference Questions," *RQ* 17 (1978): 212–22.

Ellis, D. G., "Interpersonal Deception: Theory and Critique," *Communication Theory* 6 (1996): Special issue.

Ellsion, John W., "How Approachable Are You as a Public Service Librarian?" *Unabashed Librarian,* no. 46 (1983): 4–6.

Fisher, B. Aubrey, "The Pragmatic Perspective of Human Communication: A View from Systems Theory," in *Human Communication Theory: Comparative Essays,* ed. Francis E. X. Dance (New York: Harper & Row, 1982, 192–219).

Fisher, B. Aubrey, and Adams, Katherine L., *Interpersonal Communication: Pragmatics of Human Relationships,* 2nd ed. (New York: McGraw–Hill, 1994).

Fivars, Grace, *The Critical Incident Technique: A Bibliography,* 2nd ed. (Palo Alto, Calif.: American Institute for Research in the Behavioral Sciences, 1980). ERIC Document 195 681.

Flanagan, John C., "The Critical Incident Technique," *Psychological Bulletin* 51 (July 1954): 327–58.

Gallop, R., "Interpersonal Attraction and Nursing Needs," *Nursing Papers: Perspectives in Nursing* 17 (1985): 30–40.

Genova, Bissy, *Nonverbal Behaviors in Presearch Interviews* (Bethesda, Md.: National Library of Medicine [DHEW], 1981). ERIC Document 205 188.

Gers, Ralph, and Seward, Lillie J., "Improving Reference Performance: Results of a Statewide Study," *Library Journal* 110 (Nov., 1985): 32–35.

Glogoff, Stuart, "Communication Theory's Role in the Reference Interview," *Drexel Library Quarterly* 19 (spring 1983): 56–72.

Goffman, Erving, *The Presentation of Self in Everyday Life* (Garden City, N.Y.: Doubleday Anchor, 1959).

————, *Behavior in Public Places: Notes on the Social Organization of Gatherings* (New York: Free Pr., 1963).

————, *Interaction Ritual, Essays on Face-to-Face Behavior* (Garden City, N.Y.: Anchor, 1967).

————, *Relations in Public: Microstudies of the Public Order* (New York: Basic Books, 1971).

————, *Forms of Talk* (Philadelphia: Univ. of Pennsylvania Pr., 1981).

Gothberg, Helen, "Immediacy: A Study of Communication Effect of the Reference Process," *Journal of Academic Librarianship* 2 (July 1976): 126–29.

Gothberg, Helen M., *Training Library Communication Skills: Development of 3 Video Tape Workshops* (Tuscon, Ariz.: Univ. of Arizona, 1977). ERIC Document 163 934.

Green, Samuel S., "Personal Relations between Librarians and Readers," *Library Journal* 1 (Nov., 1876): 74–81.

Greenfield, Louise, Johnston, Susan, and Williams, Karen, "Educating the World: Training Library Staff to Communicate Effectively with International Students," *Journal of Academic Librarianship* 12 (Sept. 1986): 227–31.

Gross, Melissa, "The Imposed Query," *RQ* 35 (winter 1995): 236–43.

"Guidelines for Behavioral Performance of Reference and Information Services Professionals," *RQ* 36 (winter 1996): 200–3.

Hall, A. D., and Fagen, R. E., "Definition of System," in *General Systems Theory and Human Communication*, ed. Brent D. Ruben and John Y. Kim (Rochelle Park, N.J.: Hayden, 1975), 52–65.

Hall, Patrick A., "Peanuts: A Note on Intercultural Communication," *Journal of Academic Librarianship* 18 (Sept. 1992): 211–13.

Harper, Nancy, *Human Communication Theory: The History of a Paradigm* (Rochelle Park, N.J.: Hayden, 1979).

Heinzkill, Richard, "Introducing Nonverbal Communication," *RQ* 11 (summer 1972): 356–58.

Hernon, Peter, and McClure, Charles R., "Library Reference Service: An Unrecognized Crisis—A Symposium," *Journal of Academic Librarianship* 13 (May 1987): 69–80.

Hickey, K. D., "Technostress in Libraries and Media Centers: Case Studies and Coping Strategies," *TechTrends* 37 (1992): 17–20.

Hoffmann, Irene, and Popa, Opritsa, "Library Orientation and Instruction for International Students: The University of California-Davis Experience," *RQ* 25 (spring 1986): 356–60.

Holland, Barron, "Updating Library Reference Services through Training for Interpersonal Competence," *RQ* 17 (spring 1978): 207–11.

Howell, Benita J., Reeves, Edward B., and van Willigen, John, "Fleeting Encounters—A Role Analysis of Reference Librarian–Patron Interaction," *RQ* 16 (winter 1976): 124–29.

Hutchins, Margaret. *Introduction to Reference Work* (Chicago: ALA, 1944).

Jennerich, Elaine Z., and Jennerich, Edward J., *The Reference Interview as a Creative Art,* 2nd ed. (Englewood, Colo.: Libraries Unlimited, 1997).

Katz, William, *Introduction to Reference Work*, 2nd ed. (New York: McGraw–Hill, 1974).

———, *Introduction to Reference Work,* 7th ed. (New York: McGraw-Hill, 1997).

Kazlauskas, Edward, "An Exploratory Study: A Kinesic Analysis of Academic Library Public Service Points," *Journal of Academic Librarianship* 2 (July 1976): 130–34.

Kelley, Harold H., and Thibaut, John W., *Interpersonal Relations: A Theory of Interdependence* (New York: John Wiley, 1978).

Kibirige, Harry M., "Computer-Assisted Reference Services: What the Computer Will Not Do," *RQ* 27 (spring 1988): 377–83.

King, Geraldine B., "The Reference Interview," *RQ* 12 (1972): 157–60.

Kirk, Jerome, and Miller, Marc L., *Reliability and Validity in Qualitative Research* (Beverly Hills, Calif.: Sage, 1986).

Kuhlthau, Carol C., *Seeking Meaning: A Process Approach to Library and Information Services* (Norwood, N.J.: Ablex, 1993).

Kupersmith, John, "Technostress and the Reference Librarian," *Reference Services Review* 20 (spring, 1992): 7–14+.

Lam, R. Errol, "The Reference Interview: Some Intercultural Considerations," *RQ* 27 (spring 1988): 390–95.

Lancaster, F. W., *If You Want to Evaluate Your Library . . .* (Champaign, Ill.: Univ. of Ill. Pr., 1988).

———, *If You Want to Evaluate Your Library . . .,* 2nd ed. (Champaign, Ill.: Univ. of Illinois, Graduate School of Library and Information Science, 1993).

Larason, Larry, and Robinson, Judith Schiek, "The Reference Desk: Service Point or Barrier?" *RQ* 23 (spring 1984): 332–38.

Leichter, Hope J., and Hamid-Buglione, Vera, *An Examination of Cognitive Processes in Everyday Family Life* (Columbia Univ., N.Y.: Elbenwood Center for the Study of the Family as Educator, 1983). ERIC Document 226 849.

Lewis, David W., "Making Academic Reference Services Work," *College & Research Libraries* 55 (Sept. 1994): 445–56.

Littlejohn, Stephen J., *Theories of Human Communication*, 2nd ed. (Belmont, Calif.: Wadsworth, 1983).

——, *Theories of Human Communication*, 3rd ed. (Belmont, Calif.: Wadsworth, 1989).

——, *Theories of Human Communication*, 5th ed. (Belmont, Calif.: Wadsworth, 1996).

Liu, Mengxiong, and Redfern, Bernice, "Information-Seeking Behavior of Multicultural Students: A Case Study at San Jose State University," *College & Research Libraries* 58 (July 1997): 348–54.

Liu, Ziming, "Difficulties and Characteristics of Students from Developing Countries in Using American Libraries," *College & Research Libraries* 54 (Jan. 1993): 25–31.

Lukenbill, W. Bernard, "Teaching Helping Relationship Concepts in the Reference Process," *Journal of Education for Librarianship* 18 (fall 1977): 110–20.

Lynch, Mary Jo, "Reference Interviews in Public Libraries," (Ph.D. diss., Rutgers—State Univ. of New Jersey, 1977).

Markham, Marilyn J., Stirling, Keith H., and Smith, Nathan M., "Librarian Self-Disclosure and Patron Satisfaction in the Reference Interview," *RQ* 22 (summer 1983): 369–74.

Martin, Robert, "Relational Cognition Complexity and Relational Communication in Personal Relationships," *Communication Monographs* 59 (June 1992): 150–63.

Mason, Ellsworth, and Mason, Joan, "The Whole Shebang—Comprehensive Evaluation of Reference Operations," *Reference Librarian*, no. 11 (fall/winter 1984): 25–44.

Massey-Burzio, Virginia, "Reference Encounters of a Different Kind: A Symposium," *Journal of Academic Librarianship* 18 (Nov. 1992): 276–86.

Mathews, Anne J., *Communicate! A Librarian's Guide to Interpersonal Relations* (Chicago: ALA, 1983).

McClure, Charles R., and Hernon, Peter, *Improving the Quality of Reference Service for Government Publications* (Chicago: ALA, 1983).

McCracken, Grant, *The Long Interview* (Newbury Park, Calif.: Sage, 1988).

Mehrabian, Albert, *Silent Messages* (Belmont, Calif.: Wadsworth, 1971).

Mellon, Constance A., *Naturalistic Inquiry for Library Science: Methods and Applications for Research, Evaluation, and Teaching* (New York: Greenwood, 1990).

Millar, Frank E., and Rogers, L. Edna, "A Relational Approach to Interpersonal Communication," in *Explorations in Interpersonal Communication*, ed. Gerald R. Miller (Beverly Hills, Calif.: Sage, 1976), 87–104.

Mills, C. Wright, "Situated Actions and Vocabularies of Motive," *American Sociological Review* 5 (Dec. 1940): 904–13.

Millson-Martula, Christopher, and Menon, Vanaja, "Customer Expectations: Concepts and Reality for Academic Library Services," *College & Research Libraries* 56 (Jan. 1995): 33–47.

Monge, Peter R., "The Systems Perspective as a Theoretical Basis for the Study of Human Communication," *Communication Quarterly* 25 (winter 1977): 19–29.

Mood, Terry Ann, "Foreign Students and the Academic Library," *RQ* 22 (winter 1982): 175–80.

———, "Of Sundials and Digital Watches: A Further Step toward the New Paradigm of Reference," *Reference Services Review* 22 (fall 1994): 27–32, 95.

Morris, Ruth C. T., "Toward a User-Centered Information Service," *Journal of the American Society for Information Science* 45 (Jan. 1994): 20–30.

Mount, Ellis, "Communication Barriers and the Reference Question," *Special Libraries* 57 (Oct. 1966): 575–78.

Munoz, Joanna Lopez, "The Significance of Nonverbal Communication in the Reference Interview," *RQ* 16 (spring 1977): 220–24.

Murfin, Marjorie E., and Gugelchuk, Gary M., "Development and Testing of a Reference Transaction Assessment Instrument," *College & Research Libraries* 48 (July 1987): 314–38.

Naismith, Rachael, "Reference Communication: Commonalities in the Worlds of Medicine and Librarianship," *College & Research Libraries* 57 (Jan. 1996): 44–57.

Nance-Mitchell, Veronica, "A Multicultural Library: Strategies for the Twenty-First Century," *College & Research Libraries* 57 (Sept. 1996): 405–13.

Newmyer, Jody, "The Image Problem of the Librarian: Femininity and Social Control," *Journal of Library History* 11 (Jan. 1976): 44–67.

Nielsen, Brian, "Teacher or Intermediary: Alternative Professional Models in the Information Age," *College & Research Libraries* 43 (May 1982): 183–91.

Nielsen, Brian, and Baker, Betsy, "Educating the Online Catalog User: A Model Evaluation Study," *Library Trends* 35 (spring 1987): 571–85.

Parks, Malcolm R., "Relational Communication: Theory and Research," *Human Communication Research* 3 (summer 1977): 372–81.

Pease, Kenneth, *Communication with and without Words* (Warwickshire: Vernon Scott Associates, 1974).

Peck, Theodore P., "Counseling Skills Applied to Reference Services," *RQ* 14 (spring 1975): 233–35.

Penland, Patrick R., *Communication for Librarians* (Pittsburgh: Univ. of Pittsburgh, 1971).

———, *Interpersonal Communication: Counseling, Guidance, and Retrieval for Media, Library, and Information Specialists* (New York: Dekker, 1974).

Radcliff, Carolyn J., "Interpersonal Communication with Library Patrons: Physician–Patient Research Models," *RQ* 34 (summer 1995): 497–506.

Radford, Gary P., "Positivism, Foucault, and the Fantasia of the Library: Conceptions of Knowledge and the Modern Library Experience," *Library Quarterly* 62 (Oct. 1992): 408–24.

Radford, Marie L. "Interpersonal Communication Theory in the Library Context: A Review of Current Perspectives," in *Library and Information Science Annual,* Vol. 5, ed. Bohdan S. Wynar (Englewood, Colo.: Libraries Unlimited, 1989), 3–10..

———, "Relational Aspects of Reference Interactions: A Qualitative Investigation of the Perceptions of Users and Librarians in the Academic Library" (Ph.D. diss., Rutgers—State Univ. of New Jersey, 1993).

———, "A Qualitative Investigation of Nonverbal Immediacy in the User's Decision to Approach the Academic Reference Librarian," presented at the Library Research Seminar I, Florida State Univ., Tallahassee, Fla., Nov. 1–2, 1996.

————, "Communication Theory Applied to the Reference Encounter: An Analysis of Critical Incidents," *Library Quarterly* 66 (Apr. 1996): 123–37.

Radford, Marie L., and Radford, Gary P., "Power, Knowledge, and Fear: Feminism, Foucault and the Stereotype of the Female Librarian," *Library Quarterly* 67 (July 1997): 250–66.

Rettig, James, "Reference Research Questions," *RQ* 31 (winter 1991): 167–74.

Rice, Jane, "Library-Use Instruction with Individual Users: Should Instruction Be Included in the Reference Interview?" *Reference Librarian* 10 (spring/summer 1984): 75–84.

Richardson, Joanna, "Evaluating Nonverbal Behaviour in the Reference Interview," *International Library Movement* 7 (1985): 117–23.

Richardson, John V., "Teaching General Reference Work: The Complete Paradigm and Competing Schools of Thought, 1890–1990," *Library Quarterly* 62 (Jan. 1992): 55–89.

Roethlisberger, F. J., and Dickson, William J., *Management and the Worker* (Cambridge, Mass.: Harvard Univ. Pr., 1939).

Roloff, Michael E., *Interpersonal Communication: The Social Exchange Approach* (Beverly Hills, Calif.: Sage, 1981).

Rothstein, Samuel, "Across the Desk: 100 Years of Reference Encounters," *Canadian Library Journal* 34 (1977): 391–99.

Ruben, Brent D., "The Coming of the Information Age: Information, Technology, and the Study of Behavior," in *Information and Behavior,* Vol. 1, ed. Brent D. Ruben (New Brunswick, N.J.: Transaction Bks., 1985), 3–26.

————, *Communication and Human Behavior,* 2nd ed. (New York: Macmillan, 1988).

————, "The Health Caregiver–Patient Relationship: Pathology, Etiology, Treatment," in *Communication and Health: Systems Perspective,* ed. Eileen B. Ray and Lewis Donohew (Hillsdale, N.J.: L. Erlbaum Associates, 1990), 51–68.

————, *Communicating With Patients* (Dubuque, Ia.: Kendall-Hunt, 1992).

————, "What Patients Remember: A Content Analysis of Critical Incidents in Health Care," *Health Communication* 5 (1993): 1–16.

Ruben, Brent D., and Kim, John Y., *General Systems Theory and Human Communication* (Rochelle Park, N.J.: Hayden, 1975).

Ruesch, Jurgen, and Bateson, Gregory, *Communication: The Social Matrix of Psychiatry* (New York: Norton, 1951).

Sandy, John H., "By Any Other Name, They're Still Our Customers," *American Libraries* 28 (Aug. 1997): 43–45.

Sarkodie-Mensah, Kwasi, "Dealing with International Students in a Multicultural Era," *Journal of Academic Librarianship* 18 (Sept. 1992): 214–16.

Schmidt, Janine, "Evaluation of Reference Service in College Libraries in New South Wales, Australia," in *Library Effectiveness: A State of the Art*, comp. Neil K. Kaske and William G. Jones (Chicago: ALA, 1980, 265–94).

Shannon, Claude E., and Weaver, Warren, *The Mathematical Theory of Communication* (Urbana, Ill.: Univ. of Illinois Pr., 1949).

Shavit, David, "Qualitative Evaluation of Reference Service," *Reference Librarian,* no. 11 (fall/winter 1984): 235–44.

Skiba-King, Edwina, "An Examination of the Patterns of Self-Reported Disclosure by Incest Survivors" (Ph.D. diss., Rutgers—State Univ. of New Jersey, 1993).

Stake, Jayne E., and Oliver, Joan, "Sexual Contact and Touching between Therapist and Client—A Survey of Psychologists Attitudes and Behavior," *Professional Psychology Research and Practice* 22 (Aug. 1991): 297–307.

Stalker, John C., and Murfin, Marjorie E., "Why Reference Librarians Won't Disappear: A Study of Success in Identifying Answering Sources for Reference Questions," *RQ* 35 (summer 1996): 489–503.

Stein, Barbara L., Hand, James D., and Totten, Herman L., "Understanding Preferred Cognitive Styles—A Tool for Facilitating Better Communication," *Journal of Education for Library and Information Science* 27 (summer 1986): 38–49.

Stevenson, Sally, *Performance Appraisal for Librarians: A Guided Self-Study Approach* (Albany, N.Y.: State Univ. of New York, 1980). ERIC Document 234 804.

Street, Richard L., "Interaction Processes and Outcomes in Interviews," in *Communication Yearbook* 9, ed. Margaret L. McLaughlin (Beverly Hills, Calif.: Sage, 1986), 215–50.

Swope, Mary Jane, and Katzer, Jeffrey, "Why Don't They Ask Questions?" *RQ* 12 (winter 1972): 161–66.

Taylor, Robert S., "Question Negotiation and Information Seeking in Libraries," *College & Research Libraries* 29 (May 1968): 178–94.

Tedeschi, James T., *Impression Management: Theory and Social Psychological Research* (New York: Academic Pr., 1981).

Tenopir, Carol, "Costs and Benefits of CD-ROM," *Library Journal* 112 (Sept., 1987): 156–57.

Thompson, Mark J., Smith, Nathan M., and Woods, Bonnie L., "A Proposed Model of Self-Disclosure," *RQ* 20 (winter 1980): 160–64.

Tibbetts, Pamela, "Sensitivity Training—A Possible Application for Librarianship," *Special Libraries* 65 (Dec. 1974): 493–98.

Van Slyck, Abigail A., *Free to All: Carnegie Libraries and American Culture 1890–1920* (Chicago: Univ. of Chicago Pr., 1995).

von Bertalanffy, Ludwig, "General Systems Theory: A Critical Review," *General Systems* 7 (1962): 1–20.

———, *General Systems Theory, Foundations, Developments, Applications* (New York: Braziller, 1968).

Walker, Geraldene, and Janes, Joseph, *Online Retrieval: A Dialogue of Theory and Practice* (Englewood, Colo.: Libraries Unlimited, 1993).

Walters, Suzanne, *Customer Service: A How-to-Do-It Manual For Librarians* (New York: Neal-Schuman Publishers, 1994).

Watzlawick, Paul, Beavin, Janet Helmick, and Jackson, Don D., *Pragmatics of Human Communication: A Study of Interactional Patterns, Pathologies, and Paradoxes* (New York: Norton, 1967).

Wayman, Sally G., "The International Student in the Academic Library," *Journal of Academic Librarianship* 9 (Jan. 1984): 336–41.

Webb, Eugene J., Campbell, Donald T., Schwartz, Richard D., and Sechrest, Lee, *Unobtrusive Measures: Nonreactive Research in the Social Sciences* (Chicago: Rand McNally, 1966).

Weingand, Darlene E., *Customer Service Excellence: A Concise Guide for Librarians* (Chicago: ALA, 1997).

Weiss, Kay, *The Impact of Nonverbal Communications on the Public Services Functions of Libraries* (Washington, D.C.: National Institute of Education [DHEW], 1976). ERIC Document 153 659.

White, Marilyn Domas, "Evaluation of the Reference Interview," *RQ* 25 (fall 1985): 76–84.

Whitlatch, Jo Bell, "Reference Service Effectiveness," *RQ* 30 (winter 1990): 205–20.

Wiener, Norbert, *Cybernetics, or Control and Communication in the Animal and the Machine* (Cambridge, Mass: Technology Pr., 1948).

Wilmot, William W., *Dyadic Communication*, 2nd ed. (New York: Random House, 1980).

———, *Relational Communication*, 4th ed. (New York: McGraw-Hill, 1995).

Wood, Julia T., *Relational Communication: Continuity and Change in Personal Relationships* (Belmont, Calif.: Wadsworth, 1995).

Woolsey, Lorette K., "The Critical Incident Technique: An Innovative Qualitative Method of Research," *Canadian Journal of Counseling* 20 (Oct. 1986): 242–54.

Young, Heartsill, ed., *The ALA Glossary of Library and Information Science* (Chicago: ALA, 1983).

Young, William F., "Methods for Evaluating Reference Desk Performance," *RQ* 25 (fall 1985): 69–75.

Zucherman, M., and Driver, R. E., "Telling Lies: Verbal and Nonverbal Correlates of Deception," in *Multi-channel Integrations of Nonverbal Behavior*, ed. Aron W. Siegman and Stanley Feldstein (Hillsdale, N.J.: Erlbaum, 1985), 129–48.

Index

⬥⬥ ⬥⬥ ⬥⬥ ⬥⬥ ⬥⬥ ⬥⬥ ⬥⬥ ⬥⬥ ⬥⬥

This index was created by Gary P. Radford using the *Nested Phrase Indexing System* (NEPHIS) developed by Timothy C. Craven (Anderson and Radford, 1988; Craven, 1986) as implemented in the *Information Organization through Textual Analysis* (IOTA) textual database management system developed by James D. Anderson (Anderson, 1988). In addition to subjects per se, all persons cited by the author in this book have been indexed, not only by the names of the cited authors, but also by the subjects related to the citation. Thus, these citing authors may be found not only by their names, but also under the subjects they discuss.

References

Anderson, James D. 1988. IOTA: Information Organization based on Textual Analysis. In *The library microcomputer environment: Management issues*, ed. S. S. Intner and J. A. Hannigan. Phoenix, Ariz.: Oryx Press.

Anderson, James D. and Gary P. Radford. 1988. Back of the book indexing with the Nested Phrase Indexing System (NEPHIS). *The Indexer* 16 (2), 79–84.

Craven, Timothy C. 1986. *String indexing*. Orlando, Fla.: Academic Press.